· *The* ·
# SECRET
## SYMBOL

# · The ·
# SECRET
# SYMBOL

*Edited and with an introduction by*
**Peter Blackstock**

**P**

**PROFILE BOOKS**

First published in Great Britain in 2009 by
Profile Books Ltd
3a Exmouth House
Pine Street
London EC1R 0JH
*www.profilebooks.com*

# · CONTENTS ·

# · INTRODUCTION ·

'**A**re you on the level?'

If someone's asked you this, or ever offered you a 'square deal', the chances are you've been dealing with a Freemason.

Freemasons use these phrases, as well as a number of handshakes and other signs, to identify themselves to each other. The reasons for this vary, but Masons are obliged to help their Brothers (note, there are no Sisters: all Masons are men), and many openly favour members of the fraternity over the 'profane' (i.e. non-Masons), especially in business deals.

The hidden world of Freemasonry has been a source of fascination to the uninitiated for centuries. Non-members have speculated feverishly about orgiastic and Satanic rituals, sorcery, political plots, international webs of intrigue and all manner of underhand skulduggery. While much of this is undoubtedly pure fantasy, even the most far-fetched and sensational claims are hard to disprove without inside information – hence their enduring appeal. Dan Brown's latest international bestseller, *The Lost Symbol*, explores the hidden world of Freemasonry, but leaves many questions about it unanswered. Just who are the Masons, what do they do and why do they do it?

## WHO ARE THE FREEMASONS?

According to documents published by the United Grand Lodge of England (the head Masonic organisation for the UK, whose London headquarters at Freemason's Hall on Great Queen Street in Covent Garden are partly open to the public), Freemasonry is the UK's largest secular, fraternal and charitable organisation, with more than 300,000 members and nearly 8,000 lodges throughout England and Wales, as well as 30,000 brethren overseas.

Contrary to popular belief, the Masons do not recruit: in order to become a Mason you must approach the fraternity with the names of two Masonic brethren who are willing to vouch for you. You must also meet the following four criteria:

1. You must be over 18 years of age (21 in the USA).
2. You must be law-abiding and of good character.
3. You must acknowledge belief in a Supreme Being (i.e. you must believe in a God of some sort – but Masons are not affiliated with any religion, Christian or otherwise, and in fact much Masonic doctrine actively preaches religious pluralism).

4. You must be male (while roughly equivalent organisations for women do exist, these are only affiliated groups rather than Masons proper).

There is an important distinction between 'operative' and 'speculative' masons. 'Operative' masons are manual labourers who cut and shape stone for a living, and who do not necessarily have any connection with Freemasonry. 'Speculative' masons are Freemasons, who pursue a wide variety of careers, but are usually white-collar workers. (Civil servants, headmasters, surgeons, policemen and judges are all professions traditionally associated with the fraternity.) The organisation of speculative Freemasons has been dated back to 1646, and is linked to Elias Ashmole, founder of the world-famous Ashmolean Museum in Oxford. Although the Freemasons draw upon the medieval guild of masons for many of their symbols and much of their terminology, these have a purely allegorical, symbolic meaning.

For example, the trowel that operative masons use to spread cement in the construction of walls is wielded symbolically by Freemasons to spread 'the cement of brotherly love and affection'. Similarly, Masons meet in 'lodges' that are reminiscent of medieval guild halls, and the three degrees of standard so-called 'Blue Lodge' Freemasonry (which derives its name from the ceiling of Masonic lodges, which were traditionally painted with a celestial map on a blue background) – 'Entered Apprentice', 'Fellow Craft' and 'Master Mason' – take their names from the three levels of seniority in medieval guilds.

These three ranks of Freemasonry are thought to date back to what is traditionally considered by Masons to be the first Masonic lodge: the Temple of Solomon. According to the Bible (Kings 6, 1–38), 30,000 workmen were involved in the Temple's construction, and although these numbers are intended only to give a sense of the immensity of the construction rather than to be taken as accurate figures, it is certain that a great number of stonemasons were employed to construct the building. These workers, so Masonic legend runs, were divided into three classes, equivalent to the three degrees of Freemasonry, and in order to identify themselves – particularly when receiving their wages – the workmen used complex handshakes and pass-words, which have been passed down and still form the crux of modern Freemasonry. In the ritual where a candidate is 'raised' to a Master Mason, for instance, he plays the role of a certain Hiram Abiff, the architect in charge of the construction of the Temple, whose imagined murder is acted out by each candidate for this highest rank of Masonry.

## WHAT DO THEY DO?

If you ask a Mason this question, he'll probably try to 'divert the discourse' (in other words, change the subject), as part of the Masonic obligation is to avoid betraying the secrets of the fraternity. In fact, the first lesson a Mason learns as an 'Entered Apprentice' deals solely with the importance of silence, and one of the principal Masonic mottos is 'Aude, Vide, Tace' ('See, Hear, Be Silent'). If he doesn't succeed in changing the subject, he might stress the organisation's charitable work – the United Grand Lodge of England's documentation states that in the last five years, Freemasons have raised more than £75m for a number of charities.

This kind-hearted, charitable side of Freemasonry is openly displayed. Freemasons are allowed to disclose their membership; it is merely the details of Masonic ritual that are meant to be kept hidden. Many Masons, while openly admitting their membership to their family and friends, might feel uncomfortable if the people close to them knew the details of the bizarre rituals of initiation and the often chilling symbolism that is present in the ceremonies of a Masonic lodge.

Apart from the chilling ceremonies, Freemasonry has much in common with other societies that operate on a local level. There is a strong Masonic hierarchy in each lodge, as well as on the national and international level, and Masonic members can attain a number of positions within their lodge, perhaps eventually becoming the lodge's 'Worshipful Master'. A Worshipful Master who has finished his one-year tenure (becoming what is called a 'Past Master') may choose to continue his progression up the Masonic hierarchy and run for national office at the United Grand Lodge of England.

It's unlikely that he'll ever reach the most elevated

rank, however, as all of the United Grand Lodge's previous Grand Masters have been members of the highest levels of the aristocracy or of the royal family itself. The current Grand Master, or, to give him his full title, the First Grand Principal of the Supreme Grand Chapter, is none other than Prince Edward, the Duke of Kent (Queen Elizabeth II's cousin). The Queen's husband, Prince Philip, has also been initiated as a Freemason (for a list of other famous Freemasons, see the Appendix on page 253), although he joined the fraternity only to fulfil the wish of his father-in-law, the late George VI. Prince Charles has stated that he doesn't wish to belong to 'any secret society' and the United Grand Lodge of England is currently lacking an obvious royal heir for its highest office. Perhaps the fraternity should open its doors to women and allow a future Queen the chance to lead the Masons, although there is still an unwritten rule that you can't be monarch and Grand Master at the same time.

## WHY DO THEY DO IT?

This is perhaps the greatest Masonic mystery of all. The Freemasons can perhaps best be described as a bureaucratic, hierarchical organisation rather like the Rotary Club or a parish council, crossed with an amateur dramatics society with a strong interest in religious performances, with something of the masculine atmosphere of a working man's club thrown in. Some Masons join the fraternity to 'escape' their wives; others because they believe – rightly or wrongly –that the Masons do possess hidden secrets that they hope to discover; others because the idea of dressing up and playing at being a High Priest (for Masonic rituals, while nominally secular, are nevertheless loaded with religious symbolism) has a particular appeal.

Why people invest considerable time and money – after all, those charitable donations don't come from thin air – in climbing the Masonic ladder is not entirely clear to the uninitiated, so perhaps the Masons know something we don't. Are they really hiding secrets? Is there more to the Masons than first meets the eye?

## ABOUT THIS BOOK

*The Secret Symbol* gathers a fascinating and unprecedented selection of extracts from original documents that, taken together, reveal the inner workings of Freemasonry down the ages. From detailed descriptions of the initiation rituals to key texts from significant insiders (including Benjamin Franklin, whose *The Constitutions of the Free-Masons* you'll find within these pages, as well as the notable Albert Pike, and even the celebrated nineteenth-century writer Thomas De Quincey), these documents draw back the curtain on a hidden world, offering astonishing glimpses of the reality of the Masonic tradition as practised through the ages.

As the documents show, the Masons are an organisation that can rightfully boast both an illustrious history and a part in many events that have shaped the world. You don't have to be a conspiracy theorist to understand the significance behind Washington laying the cornerstone of the Capitol building according to Masonic rites (see Chapter III), or to be chilled by the death and rebirth symbolism present in the ceremony of 'raising' a brother to the highest rank of standard 'Blue Lodge' Masonry, that of Master Mason.

The book contains a wealth of information relating to the role that Freemasonry has played in the history of the USA – some of the greatest names of the American Revolution, including Franklin, George Washington and Paul Revere, were Freemasons, as were between eight and fifteen of the men who signed the Declaration of Independence (some of them are only suspected rather than proved Freemasons). And out of the 40 signatories to the Constitution, 9 were known Masons, 13 had Masonic sympathies, and 6 later became Masons, meaning that a staggering 28 (or 70 per cent) of them were Masons or possible Masons. As if that were not enough, more than half of Washington's generals were Freemasons and the Boston Tea Party was planned at the Green Dragon Tavern, a known meeting place for the Masonic lodge of which Paul Revere was a member.

Separating fact from fiction and speculation in such a secretive world is not easy, but the invaluable original documents in *The Secret Symbol* give us a much greater understanding of the key principles and methods of Freemasonry. And as so often, the fact that is revealed may well prove far more interesting than the fiction.

## • CHAPTER I •

# Initiation

Initiation is the first step in Freemasonry. The organisation teaches that its secrets are not to be revealed to the 'profane' (i.e. to non-Masons) and brethren traditionally take a number of grisly oaths, swearing that they will not betray the Fraternity's hidden knowledge. Here is an extract from a Masonic textbook designed for candidates for initiation, called *The Masonic Manual: A Pocket Companion for the Initiated*, published in New York in 1867. The initiation ceremonies and the central tenets of Masonry have remained unchanged for centuries, and many of the primers that modern-day initiates read use the same text as this early example.

# FREEMASONRY: AN INITIATE'S GUIDE

THE

# MASONIC MANUAL

A pocket Companion for the Initiated:

CONTAINING THE

# RITUALS OF FREEMASONRY

EMBRACED IN THE DEGREES OF THE
LODGE CHAPTER AND ENCAMPMENT;

Compiled and arranged

## BY ROBERT MACOY

PAST MASTER, PAST GRAND SECRETARY, PAST GRAND
COMMANDER, GRAND RECORDER, ETC.

## Introduction

FREE-MASONRY is a MORAL ORDER, instituted by virtuous men, with the praiseworthy design of recalling to our remembrance the most sublime TRUTHS, in the midst of the most innocent and social pleasures, – founded on LIBERALITY, BROTHERLY LOVE and CHARITY. It is a beautiful SYSTEM of MORALITY, veiled in allegory and illustrated by symbols. TRUTH is its centre, – the point whence its radii diverge, point[ing] out to its disciples a correct knowledge of the Great Architect of the Universe, and the moral laws which he has ordained for their government.

A proper administration of the various ceremonies connected with our ritual is of the first importance and worthy of our serious consideration. The rites and cere-monies of Free-masonry form the distinctive peculiarity of the Institution. In their nature they are simple – in their end instructive. They naturally excite a high degree of curiosity in a newly initiated brother, and create an earnest desire to investigate their meaning, and to become acquainted with their object and design. It requires, however, both serious application and untiring diligence to ascertain the precise nature of every ceremony which our ancient brethren saw reason to adopt in the forma-tion of an exclusive system, which was to pass through the world unconnected with the religion and politics of all times, and of every people among whom it should flourish and increase. In order to preserve our ceremonies from the hand of innovation, it is essentially necessary that every officer should be thoroughly acquainted with them, and that a firm determination should exist among the craft to admit *no change*. A few words here or there may not in themselves appear of much consequence, yet, by frequent allowance, we become habituated to them, and thus open the door to evils of more serious magni-tude. There is, there can be, no safety but in a rigid adher-ence to the ancient ceremonies of the Order.

## Admission of candidates

By the regulations of the Fraternity, a candidate for the mysteries of Masonry cannot be initiated in any regular Lodge, without having been proposed at a preceding regular meeting. All applications for initiation should be made in writing, giving name, residence, age, occupation, and references.

The petition, having been read in open Lodge, is placed on file. A committee is then appointed to investigate the character and qualifications of the petitioner. If, at the next regular meeting of the Lodge, the report of the Committee be favorable, and the candidate is admitted, he is required to give his free and full assent to the following interrogations:

1. 'Do you seriously declare, upon your honor, before these gentlemen, that, unbiased by friends, and uninfluenced by mercenary motives, you freely and voluntarily offer yourself a candidate for the mysteries of Masonry?'
2. 'Do you seriously declare, upon your honor, before these gentlemen, that you are prompted to solicit the privileges of Masonry by a favorable opinion conceived of the Institution, a desire of knowledge, and a sincere wish of being serviceable to your fellow-creatures?'
3. 'Do you seriously declare, upon your honor, before these gentle men, that you will cheerfully conform to all the ancient established usages and customs of the Fraternity?'
4. 'Do you solemnly declare upon your honor that you have never petitioned any other lodge for initiation, and been rejected?'

The candidate, if no objection be urged to the contrary, is then introduced in due and ancient form.

[...]

## Ancient charges

### The private duties of Masons

Whoever would be a Mason should know how to practise all the private virtues. He should avoid all manner of intemperance or excess, which might prevent his performance of the laudable duties of his Craft, or lead him into enormities which would reflect dishonor upon the ancient Fraternity. He is to be industrious in his profession, and true to the Master he serves. He is to labor justly, and not to eat any man's bread for nought; but to pay truly for his meat and drink. What leisure his labor allows, he is to employ in studying the arts and sciences with a diligent mind, that he may the better perform all his duties to his Creator, his country, his neighbor and himself. He is to seek and acquire, as far as possible, the virtues of patience, meekness, self-denial, forbearance, and the like, which give him the command over himself, and enable him to govern his own family with affection, dignity and prudence: at the same time checking every disposition injurious to the world and promoting that love and service which Brethren of the same household owe to each other. Therefore, to afford succor to the distressed, to divide our bread with the industrious poor, and to put the misguided traveler into the way, are duties of the Craft, suitable to its dignity and expressive of its usefulness. But, though a Mason is never to shut his ear unkindly against the complaints of any of the human race, yet when a Brother is oppressed or suffers, he is in a more peculiar manner called upon to open his whole soul in love and compassion to him, and to relieve him without prejudice, according to his capacity.

It is also necessary, that all who would be true Masons should learn to abstain from all malice, slander and evil speaking; from all provoking, reproachful and ungodly language; keeping always a tongue of good report.

A Mason should know how to obey those who are set over him; however inferior they may be in worldly rank or condition. For although Masonry divests no man of his honors and titles, yet, in a Lodge, pre-eminence of virtue, and knowledge in the art, is considered as the true source of all nobility, rule and government.

The virtue indispensably requisite in Masons is — SECRECY. This is the guard of their confidence, and the security of their trust. So great a stress is to be laid upon it, that it is enforced under the strongest obligations; nor, in their esteem, is any man to be accounted wise who has not intellectual strength and ability sufficient to cover and conceal such honest secrets as are committed to him, as well as his own more serious and private affairs.

## Duties as citizens

A Mason is a peaceable citizen, and is never to be concerned in plots and conspiracies against the peace and welfare of the nation, nor to behave himself undutifully to inferior magistrates. He is cheerfully to conform to every lawful authority; to uphold on every occasion, the interest of the community, and zealously promote the prosperity of his own country. Masonry has ever flourished in times of peace, and been always injured by war, bloodshed and confusion; so that kings and princes in every age, have been much disposed to encourage the craftsmen on account of their peaceableness and loyalty, whereby they practically answer the cavils of their adversaries and promote the honor of the Fraternity. Craftsmen are bound by peculiar ties to promote peace, cultivate harmony, and live in concord and Brotherly Love.

## Duties in the Lodge

While the Lodge is open for work, Masons must hold no private conversation or committees without leave from the Master; nor talk of anything foreign or impertinent; nor interrupt the Master or Wardens, or any Brother addressing himself to the Chair; nor behave inattentively, while the Lodge is engaged in what is serious and solemn; but every Brother shall pay due reverence to the Master, the Wardens, and all his fellows. Every Brother guilty of a fault shall submit to the Lodge, unless he appeal to the Grand Lodge.

No private offences, or disputes about nations, families, religions or politics, must be brought within the doors of the Lodge.

## Duties as neighbors

Masons ought to be moral men. Consequently they should be good husbands, good parents, good sons and good neighbors; avoiding all excess injurious to themselves or families, and wise as to all affairs, both of their own household and of the Lodge, for certain reasons known to themselves.

## Duties towards a Brother

Free and Accepted Masons have ever been charged to avoid all slander of true and faithful Brethren, and all malice or unjust resentment, or talking disrespectfully of a Brother's person or performance. Nor must they suffer any to spread unjust reproaches or calumnies against a Brother behind his back, nor to injure him in his fortune, occupation or character; but they shall defend such a Brother, and give him notice of any danger or injury wherewith he may be threatened, to enable him to escape the same, as far as is consistent with honor, prudence, and the safety of religion, morality, and the state; but no farther.

## INSIDE THE LODGE:
## THE RITUALS REVEALED

In the opening pages of *The Lost Symbol*, Dan Brown describes a fundamental Masonic ritual: the raising of a Masonic brother to the highest rank of Scottish Rite Masonry (see Chapter VI), the 33rd degree. Masonic initiation ceremonies – rolling up one trouser leg, giving each other strange handshakes, etc. – are often the subject of jokes among outsiders, but the strange reality of these ceremonies is often rather disturbing. *Duncan's Ritual and Monitor of Freemasonry* (1867) was among the first books to expose the initiation ceremonies of the three degrees of Blue Lodge Masonry: Entered Apprentice, Fellow Craft, and Master Mason.

# DUNCAN'S RITUAL AND MONITOR OF FREEMASONRY

## Entered Apprentice, or First Degree

Seven Freemasons, viz., six Entered Apprentices and one Master Mason, acting under a charter or dispensation from some Grand Lodge, is the requisite number to constitute a Lodge of Masons, and to initiate a candidate to the First Degree of Masonry.

They assemble in a room well guarded from all cowans and eaves-droppers, in the second or third story (as the case may be) of some building suitably prepared and furnished for Lodge purposes, which is, by Masons, termed "the Ground Floor of King Solomon's Temple."

The officers take their seats, as represented here.

At the time of receiving a petition [from a candidate for initiation] for the degrees of Masonry, the Master appoints a committee of three, whose duty it is to make inquiry after the character of the applicant, and report good or bad, as the case may be, at the next regular meeting, when it is acted upon by the Lodge.

Upon reception of the committee's report, a ballot is had: if no black balls appear, the candidate is declared duly elected; but if one black ball or more appear, he is declared rejected.

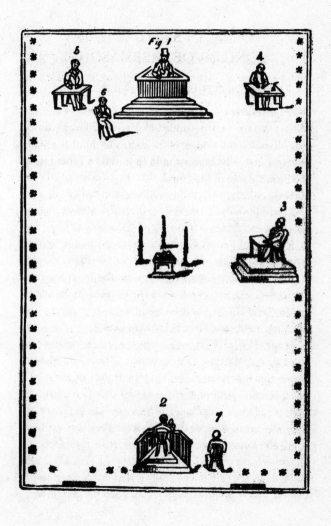

[...]

[W]hen a candidate is initiated to the First Degree, he is styled as "entered;" when he has taken the Second Degree, "passed" and when he has taken the Third, "raised" to the sublime Degree of a Master Mason. No one is allowed to be present, in any degree of Masonry, except he be one of that same degree or higher. The Master always wears his hat when presiding as such, but no other officer in a "Blue Lodge" (a *"Blue Lodge"* is a Lodge of Master Masons, where only three degrees are conferred, viz.: Entered Apprentice, 1st; Fellow Craft, 2d; Master Mason, 3d. Country Lodges are mostly all *"Blue Lodges"*).

A Lodge of Fellow Craft Masons consists of five, viz.: Worshipful Master, Senior and Junior Wardens, Senior and Junior Deacons; yet seven besides the Tyler generally assist, and take their seats as in the Entered Apprentice's Degree. The Fellow Craft Lodge is styled by Masons "the Middle Chamber of King Solomon's Temple."

Three Master Masons is the requisite number to constitute a Masters' Lodge, which is called by Masons *"the Sanctum Sanctorum, or, Holy of Holies of King Solomon's Temple."* Although three are all that is required by "Masonic Law" to open a Third Degree Lodge, there are generally seven besides the Tyler, as in the other degrees.

All the Lodges meet in one room, alike furnished, for the conferring of the different degrees (E. A., F. C., and M. M.); but they are masonically styled by the Craft as the Ground Floor, Middle Chamber, and *Sanctum Sanctorum*.

A person being in the room, while open on the First Degree, would not see any difference in the appearance of the room from a Master Masons' Lodge. It is the duty of the Tyler to inform all the brethren on what degree the Lodge is at work, especially those that arrive too late (*i.e.*, after the Lodge has been opened), so that none will be liable to give the wrong sign to the Worshipful Master when he enters. If the Lodge is opened on the First Degree, there might be present those who had taken only one degree, and, if the brother arriving late should be ignorant of this fact, and make a Third Degree sign, they would see it; consequently, caution on this point should always be given to such brethren by the Tyler, before entering the Lodge.

Usual way: Brethren that arrive too late come up to the ante-room, which they find occupied by the Tyler, sword in hand; after inquiring of the Tyler on what degree the Lodge is at work (opened), they put on an apron, and request the Tyler to let them in; the Tyler steps to the door, gives one rap (•), *i.e.* if opened on the First Degree; two raps (• •), if Second Degree; three raps (• • •), if the Third Degree; which being heard by the Junior Deacon, on the inside, he reports to the Master the alarm, as follows, viz.:

J. D.--Worshipful Master, there is an alarm at the inner door of our Lodge.

On the evening of a Lodge-meeting, brethren generally get together at an early hour at the Lodge-room, which has been opened and cleaned out by the Tyler. On arrival of the Master, and the hour of meeting, the Master repairs to his seat in the east, puts on his *hat*, sash, yoke, and apron, with gavel in hand, and says: "Brethren will be properly clothed and in order; officers repair to their stations for the purpose of opening."

[...]

W. M.--Brother Senior Deacon, you will attend at the altar. (Here the Senior Deacon steps to the altar, places the square above the compasses, if opened on the First Degree.)

W. M. (gives one sound of the gavel)--All are seated and ready for business.

[...]

## THE RITUALS REVEALED: ENTERED APPRENTICE

W. M. (disposing of such other business as may lawfully come before the Lodge)--Brethren, if there is no further business before this Lodge of Master Masons, we will proceed to close the same, and open an Entered Apprentices' Lodge, for the purpose of initiation. [...]

W. M.--Brother Senior Warden, are you sure all present are Entered Apprentice Masons?

S. W.--I am sure, Worshipful, all present are Entered Apprentice Masons.

*Duegard of an Entered Apprentice*

W. M.--If you are sure all present are Entered Apprentice Masons, you will have them come to order as such, reserving yourself for the last.

S. W. (gives three raps with his gavel, all rise to their feet) --Brethren, you will come to order as Entered Apprentice Masons.

The members place their hands in the position of a duegard of an Entered Apprentice (see figure above). When the Master makes the sign, by drawing his hand across his throat (see figure on following page), all follow suit; Worshipful then makes one rap with the gavel, Senior Warden one, and the Junior Warden one.

W. M.--[...] Brother Junior Deacon, you will take with you the necessary assistants (the two Stewards), repair to the ante-room, where there is a candidate in waiting

*Sign of an Entered Apprentice*

(Mr. Gabe, for the First Degree in Masonry), and, when duly prepared, you will make it known by the usual sign (one rap).

Secretary [to candidate]--Do you seriously declare, upon your honor, that, unbiased by friends, and uninfluenced by mercenary motives, you freely and voluntarily offer yourself a candidate for the mysteries of Masonry?

--Yes (or, I do).

--Do you seriously declare, upon your honor, that you are prompted to solicit the privileges of Masonry by a favorable opinion of the institution, a desire for knowledge, and a sincere wish of being serviceable to your fellow-creatures?

--Yes.

--Do you seriously declare, upon your honor, that you

*Entered Apprentice duly and truly prepared*

will conform to all the ancient usages of the Order?

--Yes.

The Secretary returns to the Lodge, and reports that the candidate has given his assent to the interrogations. The candidate is now requested to strip.

J. D.--Mr. Gabe, you will take off your coat, shoes, and stockings, also your vest and cravat; and now your pantaloons; here is a pair of drawers for you. You will now slip your left arm out of your shirt-sleeve, and put it through the bosom of your shirt, that your arm and breast may be naked.

The Deacon now ties a handkerchief or hoodwink over his eyes, places a slipper on his right foot, and afterwards puts a rope, called a cable-tow, once round his neck, letting it drag behind.

The previous figure is a representation of the candidate duly and truly prepared for the First Degree in Masonry.

The Junior Deacon now takes the candidate by the arm and leads him forward to the door of the Lodge, and gives three distinct knocks, when the Senior Deacon, on the inside, rises to his feet, makes the sign of an Entered Apprentice to the Master, and says:

S. D.--Worshipful Master, there is an alarm at the inner door of our Lodge.

W. M.--You will attend to the alarm, and ascertain the cause. (The Deacon repairs to the door, gives three distinct knocks, and then opens it.)

S. D.--Who comes here?

J. D. (who always responds for the candidate)--Mr. Peter Gabe, who has long been in darkness, and now seeks to be brought to light, and to receive a part in the rights and benefits of this worshipful Lodge, erected to God, and dedicated to the holy Sts. John, as all brothers and fellows have gone before.

S. D.--Mr. Gabe, is it of your own free-will and accord?

Mr. G.--It is.

S. D.--Brother Junior Deacon, is he worthy, and well qualified?

J. D.--He is.

S. D.--Duly and truly prepared?

J. D.--He is.

S. D.--Of lawful age, and properly vouched for?

J. D.--He is.

S. D.--By what further right or benefit does he expect to gain admission?

J. D.--By being a man, free born, of good repute, and well recommended.

S. D.--Is he such?

J. D.--He is.

S. D.--Since he is in possession of all these necessary qualifications, you will wait with patience until the Worshipful Master is informed of his request, and his answer returned.

Deacon closes the door and repairs to the altar before the Worshipful Master, raps once on the floor with his rod, which is responded to by the Master with his gavel, when the same thing is passed through with as at the door, and the Master says:

W. M.--Let him enter, and be received in due form.

The Senior Deacon takes the compasses from off the altar, repairs to the door, opens it, and says:

S. D.--Let him enter, and be received in due form.

Senior Deacon steps back, while the Junior Deacon, with candidate, enters the Lodge, followed by the two Stewards. As they advance they are stopped by the Senior Deacon, who presents one point of the compasses to the candidate's naked left breast, and says:

S. D.--Mr. Gabe, on entering this Lodge for the first time, I receive you on the point of a sharp instrument pressing your naked left breast, which is to teach you, as it is a torture to your flesh, so should the recollection of it ever be to your mind and conscience, should you attempt to reveal the secrets of Masonry unlawfully.

The Junior Deacon now leaves the candidate in the hands of the Senior Deacon, and takes his seat at the right hand of the Senior Warden in the west; while the Senior Deacon, followed by the two Stewards, proceeds to travel once regularly around the Lodge-room, as follows, viz.: Senior Deacon takes the candidate by the right arm, advances a step or two, when the Master gives one rap with his gavel. (Deacon and candidate stop.)

W. M.--Let no one enter on so important a duty without first invoking the blessing of the Deity. Brother Senior Deacon, you will conduct the candidate to the centre of the Lodge, and cause him to kneel for the benefit of prayer.

S. D.--Mr. Gabe, you will kneel. (Candidate kneels.)

Worshipful Master now leaves his seat in the east, approaches candidate, kneels by his side, and repeats the following prayer, viz.:--

W. M.--Vouchsafe Thine aid, Almighty Father of the Universe, to this our present convention; and grant that this candidate for Masonry may dedicate and devote his life to Thy service, and become a true and faithful brother among us! Endue him with a competency of Thy divine wisdom, that, by the secrets of our art, he may be better enabled to display the beauties of brotherly love, relief, and truth, to the honor of Thy Holy Name. Amen.

Responded to by all, "So mote it be."

W. M. (rising to his feet, taking candidate by the right hand, placing his left on his head)--"Mr. Gabe" (sometimes Masters say, "Stranger!"), in whom do you put your trust?

Candidate (prompted)--In God.

W. M.--Since in God you put your trust, your faith is well founded. Arise (assists candidate to rise), follow your conductor and fear no danger.

The Master retires to his seat in the east, and while the conductor (S. D.) is attending the candidate once around the Lodge-room, [...] as they pass each officer's station, east, south, and west, they give one sound with their gavels, viz.: first the Master, one (•): J. W., one (•); S. W., one (•); which has a good effect on the candidate, the sounds being near his ears as he passes by (his conductor generally passing close up). Having passed once around the Lodge, they halt at the Junior Warden's station in the south.

J. W. (gives one rap; conductor one)--Who comes here?

Conductor (S. D.)--Mr. Peter Gabe, who has long been in darkness, and now seeks to be brought to light, and to receive a part in the rights and benefits of this Worshipful Lodge, erected to God, and dedicated to the holy St. John, as all brothers and fellows have done before.

J. W.--Mr. Gabe, is it of your own free will and accord?

Mr. Gabe--It is.

J. W.--Brother Senior Deacon, is he worthy and well qualified?

S. D.--He is.

J. W.--Duly and truly prepared?

S. D.--He is.

J. W.--Of lawful age, and properly vouched for?

S. D.--He is.

J. W.--By what further right or benefit does he expect to gain admission?

S. D.--By being a man, free born, of good repute, and well recommended.

J. W.--Since he is in possession of all these necessary qualifications, I will suffer him to pass on to the Senior Warden's station in the west.

Senior Warden, disposing of him in the same manner as the Junior Warden, suffers him to pass on to the Worshipful Master in the east, who makes the same inquiries as did the Wardens in the south and west, after which the Master says:

W. M.--From whence come you, and whither are you traveling?

S. D.--From the west, and traveling toward the east.

W. M.--Why leave you the west and travel toward the east?

S. D.--In search of light.

W. M.--Since light is the object of your search, you will reconduct the candidate, and place him in charge of the Senior Warden in the west, with my orders that he teach this candidate to approach the east, the place of light, by advancing with one upright, regular step to the first stop, the heel of his right placed in the hollow of his left foot, his body erect at the altar, before the Worshipful Master in the east.

Senior Deacon conducts candidate back to the Senior Warden in the west, and says:

S. D.--Brother Senior Warden, it is the orders of the Worshipful Master that you teach this candidate to approach the east, the place of light, by advancing on one regular upright step to the first stop; the heel of his right foot in the hollow of his left, his body erect at the altar before the Worshipful Master in the east.

Senior Warden leaves his seat, comes down to the candidate, faces him towards the Worshipful Master, and requests him to step off with his left foot, bringing the heel of his right in the hollow of his left. Before the candidate is requested to do this, he is led by the Warden within one pace of the altar. Senior Warden reports to the Worshipful Master.

S. W.--The candidate is in order, and awaits your further will and pleasure.

The Master now leaves his seat in the east, and, approaching (in front of the altar) the candidate, says:

W. M.--Mr. Gabe, before you can be permitted to advance any farther in Masonry, it becomes my duty to inform you, that you must take upon yourself a solemn oath or obligation, appertaining to this degree, which I, as Master of this Lodge, assure you will not materially interfere with the duty that you owe to your God, yourself, family, country, or neighbor. Are you willing to take such an oath?

Candidate--I am.

W. M.--Brother Senior Warden, you will place the candidate in due form, which is by kneeling on his naked left knee, his right forming the angle of a square, his left hand supporting the Holy Bible, square, and compasses, his right hand resting thereon.

The Warden now places, or causes the candidate to be placed, in the position commanded by the Worshipful Master.

W. M.--Mr. Gabe, you are now in position for taking upon yourself the solemn oath of an Entered Apprentice Mason, and, if you have no objections still, you will say I, and repeat your name after me.

Master gives one rap with his gavel which is the signal for all present to assemble around the altar.

## Obligation

I, Peter Gabe, of my own free will and accord, in the presence of Almighty God, and this Worshipful Lodge, erected to Him, and dedicated to the holy *Sts. John*, do hereby and hereon (Master presses his gavel on candidate's knuckles) most solemnly and sincerely promise and swear that I will always *hail*, ever conceal, and never reveal, any of the arts, parts, or points of the hidden mysteries of Ancient Free Masonry, which may have been, or hereafter shall be, at this time, or any future period, communicated to me, as such, to any person or persons whomsoever, except it be to a true and lawful brother Mason, or in a regularly constituted Lodge of Masons; nor unto him or them until, by strict trial, due examination, or lawful information, I shall have found him, or them, as lawfully entitled to the same as I am myself. I furthermore promise and swear that I will not print, paint, stamp, stain, cut, carve, mark, or engrave them, or cause the same to be done, on any thing movable or immovable, capable of receiving the least impression of a word, syllable, letter, or character, whereby the same may become legible or intelligible to any person under the canopy of heaven, and the secrets of Masonry thereby unlawfully obtained through my unworthiness.

All this I most solemnly, sincerely promise and swear, with a firm and steadfast resolution to perform the same, without any mental reservation or secret evasion of mind whatever, binding myself under no less penalty than that of having my throat cut across, my tongue torn out by its roots, and *my body buried in the rough sands of the sea*, at low-water mark, where the tide ebbs and flows twice in twenty-four hours, should I ever knowingly violate this my Entered Apprentice obligation. So help me God, and keep me steadfast in the due performance of the same.

W. M.--In token of your sincerity, you will now detach your hands, and kiss the book on which your hands rest, which is the Holy Bible.

After the candidate has kissed the Bible, he is asked by the Master:

W. M.--In your present condition, what do you most desire?

Candidate (prompted)--*Light*.

W. M.--Brethren, you will stretch forth your hands, and assist me in bringing our newly made brother to light.

Here the brethren surrounding the altar place their hands in form of duegard of an Entered Apprenticed Mason (figure, page 25).

W. M.--"In the beginning God created the heavens and the earth. And the earth was without form, and void; and darkness was upon the face of the waters. And God said, Let there be light, and there was light." (In some Lodges, at the last word, "light," the brethren stamp their feet and clap their hands once; but this is nearly done away with nowadays. […])

Worshipful Master now gives one rap which is the signal for all to be seated but himself, he remaining at the altar. I should remark here, that at the word "light," the conductor strips off the hoodwink from the candidate's eyes, but keeps him yet kneeling at the altar.

W. M.--Brother Senior Deacon, I will now thank you to remove the cable-tow. (Rope is taken off candidate's neck.)

Some Masters say, "As we now hold the brother by a stronger tie."

W. M.--My brother, on being brought to light in this degree, you discover both points of the compasses hid by the square, which is to signify that you are yet in darkness as respects Masonry, you having only received the degree of an Entered Apprentice. You also discover the three great lights of Masonry, by the help of the three lesser. The three great lights in Masonry are the Holy Bible, square, and compasses, which are thus explained: the Holy Bible is the rule and guide of our faith and practice; the square, to square our actions; the compasses, to circumscribe and keep us within bounds with all mankind, but more especially with a brother Mason. The three lesser lights are the three burning tapers which you see placed in a triangular form about this altar. They represent the sun, moon, and Master of the Lodge; and as the sun rules the day, and the moon governs the night, so ought the Worshipful Master to endeavor to rule and govern his Lodge, with equal regularity.

W. M. (taking a step back from the altar)--You next discover me as the Master of this Lodge, approaching you from the east, under the duegard, sign, and step of an Entered Apprentice Mason (Master making the duegard, sign, and step, as represented and explained in the figure

*Grip of an Entered Apprentice Mason*

on page 25) and, in token of my brotherly love and favor, present you my right hand (takes the candidate by the right hand, who is yet kneeling at the altar), and with it the grip and word of an Entered Apprentice. (W. M. to candidate)--Grip me, brother, as I grip you. As you are yet uninformed, your conductor will answer for you. (Senior Deacon.)

W. M. (looking the Deacon in the eye, while holding candidate by the right hand)--I hail.

S. D.--I conceal.

W. M.--What do you conceal?

S. D.--All the secrets of Masons, in Masons, to which this (here presses his thumb-nail on the joint [as in the figure above]) token alludes.

W. M.--What is that?

S. D.--A grip.

W. M.--Of what?

S. D.--Of an Entered Apprentice Mason.

W. M.--Has it a name?

S. D.--It has.

W. M.--Will you give it me?

S. D.--I did not so receive it; neither can I so impart it.

W. M.--How will you dispose of it?

S. D.--I will letter it, or halve it.

W. M.--Letter it, and begin.

S. D.--No, you begin.

W. M.--Begin you.

S. D.--A.

W. M.--B.

S. D.--O.

W. M.--Z.

S. D.--Bo.

W. M.--Az.

S. D. (pronouncing)--Boaz. [(In spelling this word--Boaz--always begin with the letter "A." This is one way that Masons detect impostors, *i.e.*, [...] book Masons.)]

W. M. (helping candidate to rise from the altar, by the right hand)--Rise, my brother, and salute the Junior and Senior Wardens as an obligated Entered Apprentice.

Here Lodges differ; some only pass [the] candidate once around the room, and, as he passes the officers' stations, he gives the duegard and sign of an Entered Apprentice; while other Lodges require him to halt at the Wardens' stations, and pass through with the [same] ceremony [once more] [...]

J. W.--I am satisfied, and will suffer you to pass on to the Senior Warden in the west for his examination.

The conductor and candidate pass on to the Senior Warden's station, where the same ceremony is gone through with, and suffers them to pass on to the Worshipful Master in the east. As they leave the west, and are nearly to the Master's station in the east, he gives one rap with his gavel, when they halt. The Master takes a white linen apron (sometimes a lambskin, which is kept for such purposes), approaches the candidate, hands it to him rolled up, and says:

W. M.--Brother, I now present you with a lambskin or white apron, which is an emblem of innocence and the badge of a Mason, more ancient than the Golden Fleece or Roman Eagle, and, when worthily worn, more honorable than the Star and Garter, or any other order that can be conferred on you at this time, or any future period, by kings, princes, and potentates, or any other persons, except it be by Masons. I trust that you will wear it with equal pleasure to yourself and honor to the fraternity. You will carry it to the Senior Warden in the west, who will teach you how to wear it as an Entered Apprentice.

Deacon conducts candidate back to the west, and says:

S. D.--Brother Senior Warden, it is the order of the Worshipful Master that you teach this new-made brother how to wear his apron as an Entered Apprentice.

The Senior Warden takes the apron and ties it on the candidate, with the flap turned up, remarking to the

candidate as he does so: This is the way, Brother Gabe,
that Entered Apprentices wore their aprons at the building of King Solomon's Temple, and so you will wear yours
until further advanced.

Senior Deacon now reconducts the candidate to the
Worshipful Master in the east.

W. M.--Brother Gabe, agreeably to an ancient custom,
adopted among Masons, it is necessary that you should
be requested to deposit something of a metallic kind or
nature, not for its intrinsic valuation, but that it may be
laid up among the relics in the archives of this Lodge, as a
memento that you were herein made a Mason. Anything,
brother that you may have about you, of a metallic nature,
will be thankfully received--a button, pin, five or ten cent
piece--anything, my brother.

Candidate feels for something--becomes quite confused. On examination, or reflection, finds himself very
destitute, not being able to contribute one pin, his conductor having been careful to take every thing from him,
in the ante-room, before he entered the Lodge;--finally
stammers out that he has nothing of the kind with him,
but if permitted to pass out into the ante-room, where his
clothes are, he will contribute. This the Master refuses
to do, of course, which only helps confuse the candidate
more and more. After the Master has kept the candidate
in this suspense some moments, he says:

W. M.--Brother Gabe, you are indeed an object of charity--
almost naked, not one cent, no, not even a button or pin

to bestow on this Lodge. Let this ever have, my brother, a lasting effect on your mind and conscience; and remember, should you ever see a friend, but more especially a brother, in a like destitute condition, you will contribute as liberally to his support and relief as his necessities may seem to demand and your ability permit, without any material injury to yourself or family.

W. M.--Brother Senior Deacon, you will now reconduct this candidate to the place from whence he came, and reinvest him with that which he has been divested of, and return him to the Lodge for further instruction.

Senior Deacon takes candidate by the arm, leads him to the centre of the Lodge, at the altar before the Worshipful Master in the east, makes duegard and sign of an Entered Apprentice, and then retires to the ante-room.

After candidate is clothed, the deacon ties on his apron, and, returning to the Lodge, conducts him to the Worshipful Master in the east, who orders the Deacon to place him in the northeast corner of the Lodge, which is at the Master's right.

W. M.--Brother Gabe, you now stand in the northeast corner of this Lodge, as the youngest Entered Apprentice, an upright man and Mason, and I give it to you strictly in charge as such ever to walk and act. (Some Masters preach great sermons to candidate on this occasion.) Brother, as you are clothed as an Entered Apprentice, it is necessary you should have the working-tools of an Entered Apprentice, which are the twenty-four-inch gauge and common gavel.

W. M.--The twenty-four-inch gauge is an instrument made use of by operative masons to measure and lay out their work; but we, as Free and Accepted Masons, are taught to make use of it for the more noble and glorious purpose of dividing our time. It being divided into twenty-four equal parts, is emblematical of the twenty-four hours of the day which we are taught to divide into three parts, whereby we find a portion for the service of God and the relief of a distressed worthy brother, a portion for our usual avocations, and a portion for refreshment and sleep.

W. M.--The common gavel is an instrument made use of by operative masons to break off the superfluous corners of rough stones, the better to fit them for the builder's use; but we, as Free and Accepted Masons, are taught to make use of it for the more noble and glorious purpose of divesting our minds and consciences of all the vices and superfluities of life, thereby fitting us, as living stones, for that spiritual building, that house not made with hands, eternal in the heavens.

# THE RITUALS REVEALED:
# FELLOW CRAFT

## Fellow Craft, or Second Degree

I shall omit the ceremonies incident to opening a Lodge of

*Duegard of a Fellow Craft Mason*

Fellow Crafts, as they are very similar to those employed in opening the First Degree, and will be explained hereafter more clearly to the reader. […]

We will suppose the Lodge to be opened on the Fellow Craft Degree, and Mr. Gabe, who has previously taken the degree of Entered Apprentice, and been elected to that of Fellow Craft, is in the ante-room in waiting. The Master, being aware of this fact, will say:

W. M.--Brother Junior Deacon, you will take with you the necessary assistance and repair to the ante-room, where there is a candidate in waiting for the Second Degree in Masonry; and when you have him prepared, make it known by the usual sign.

The Junior Deacon, with the two Stewards accompanying him, steps to the centre of the Lodge, makes the duegard and sign of a Fellow Craft, and passes out of

*Sign of a Fellow Craft Mason*

the Lodge into the ante-room. (For duegard and sign see figures above.)

J. D.--Well, Brother Gabe, you will have to be prepared for this Degree as all have been before you. You, of course, can have no serious objection?

Brother Gabe--I have not.

J. D.--Then you will take off your boots, coat, pants, vest, necktie, and collar; and here is a pair of drawers, unless you have a pair of your own. Now you will slip your right arm out of your shirtsleeve, and put it through the bosom of your shirt, that your right arm and breast may be naked.

The Deacon here ties a hoodwink, or hand-kerchief, over both eyes. [...] The Junior Deacon then ties a rope, by Masons called a cable-tow, twice around his arm. (Formerly, the rope was put twice round the candidate's

*Fellow Craft duly and truly prepared*

neck.) Some Lodges follow the old custom now, but this is rather a rare thing. The reader will, however, do well to recollect these hints, as they are particular points.

The right foot and knee of the candidate are made bare by rolling up the drawers, and a slipper should be put on his left foot. This being accomplished, the candidate is duly and truly prepared (see figure, above).

The Deacon now takes the candidate by the arm, and leads him forward to the door of the Lodge; and upon arriving there he gives three raps, when the Senior Deacon, who has taken his station on the inside door of the Lodge, reports to the Master as follows:

S. D.--Worshipful Master (making the sign of a Fellow Craft), there is an alarm at the inner door of our Lodge.

W. M.--You will attend to the alarm, and ascertain the cause.

[...]

J. W. (giving two raps, which are responded to by the deacon)--Who comes here?

S. D. (conductor)--Brother Gabe, who has been regularly initiated Apprentice, and now wishes to receive more light in Masonry, by being passed to the Degree of Fellow Craft.

J. W. (turning to candidate)--Brother Gabe, is it of your own free-will and accord?

Candidate--It is.

J. W.--Brother Senior Deacon, is he duly and truly prepared, worthy, and well qualified?

S D.--He is.

J. W.--Has he made suitable proficiency in the preceding Degree?

S. D.--He has.

J. W.--And properly vouched for?

S. D.--He is.

J. W.--Who vouches for him?

S. D.--A brother.

J. W.--By what further right, or benefit does he expect to gain admission?

S. D.--By the benefit of the pass.

J. W.--Has he that pass?

S. D.--He has it not, but I have it for him.

J. W.--Advance, and give me the pass.

Senior Deacon advances, and whispers in the Junior Warden's ear, "Shibboleth."

J. W.--The pass is right; I will suffer you to pass on to the Senior Warden's station in the west. [...]

W. M.--The pass is right; from whence came you, and whither are you traveling?

S. D.--From the west, traveling toward the east.

W. M.--Why leave you the west, and travel toward the east?

S. D.--In search of more light.

W. M.--Since that appears to be the object of the candidate's search, it is my orders that he be reconducted to the Senior Warden in the west, who will teach him how to approach the east, by two upright regular steps, his feet forming an angle of a square, his body erect at the altar before the Worshipful Master in the east.

Senior Deacon conducts the candidate back to the Senior Warden in the west, and says:

S. D.--Brother Senior Warden, it is the orders of the Worshipful Master that you teach this candidate to approach the east, by two upright regular steps, his feet forming an angle of a square, his body erect at the altar before the Worshipful Master in the east.

Senior Warden leaves his seat, and, approaching the candidate, he leads him toward the altar, and within two steps of it, and says:

Brother, you will first step off one full step with your left foot, bringing the heel of your right in the hollow of your left foot, now you will step off with your right foot, bringing the heel of your left in the hollow of your right.

The candidate is now within kneeling distance of the altar, and the Senior Warden makes the following report to the Master:--

Worshipful Master, the candidate is now in order, and awaits your further will and pleasure.

W. M.--Brother Senior Warden, you will place him in due form for taking upon himself the solemn oath or obligation of a Fellow Craft.

The Senior Warden, with the assistance of the Senior Deacon, now causes the candidate to kneel on his naked right knee, before the altar, making his left knee form a square. His left arm, as far as the elbow, should be held in a horizontal position, and the rest of the arm in a vertical position, forming another square--his arm supported by the square, held under his elbow, and his right hand resting on the open Bible.

W. M.--Brother Gabe, you are kneeling for the second time at the sacred altar of Masonry, to take upon yourself the solemn oath or obligation of a Fellow Craft; and I take pleasure, as Master of this Lodge, to say to you (as on a former occasion), there is nothing in this oath that will interfere with the duty that you owe to your God, your family, country, neighbor, or self. Are you willing to take it?

Candidate--I am.

W. M.--Then, if you have no objections, you will say, I, and repeat your name after me (here the Master gives two raps with his gavel (• •), which is the signal for all the brethren to assemble around the altar:

## Oath

[Ed.: The oath is the same as before, with a few minor additions.]

All this I most solemnly promise and swear with a firm and steadfast resolution to perform the same, without any hesitation, mental reservation, or self-evasion of mind whatever, binding myself under no less penalty than of having my breast torn open, my heart plucked out, and placed on the highest pinnacle of the temple, there to be devoured by the vultures of the air, should I ever knowingly violate the Fellow Craft obligation. So help me God, and keep me steadfast in the due performance of the same.

W. M.--Brother Gabe, you will detach your hand, and kiss the book on which your hand rests, which is the Holy Bible.

Candidate kisses the book once (some Lodges say twice).

W. M.--In your present condition, what do you most desire?

The candidate, prompted by his conductor, answers--More light in Masonry.

W. M.--Brethren, you will stretch forth your hands, and assist me in bringing our brother to light.

Here all the brethren place their hands in the form of the duegard of a Fellow Craft (see figure, page 44).

W. M.--Let the brother receive light.

At this point the conductor unties the hoodwink, and lets it fall from the candidate's eyes. The Master then gives one rap on the altar with his gavel, when all the brethren but himself and the conductor (S. D.) take their seats. The Master then says to the candidate:

W. M.--My brother, on being brought to light in this Degree, you behold one point of the compasses elevated above the square, which is to signify that you have received light in Masonry by points.

Then, stepping back a few feet from the altar, the Worshipful Master continues:

W. M.--Brother, you discover me approaching you from the east, under the duegard (here he makes the duegard) and sign (here he makes the sign of a Fellow Craft); and in token of the continuance of brotherly love and favor, I present you with my right hand (takes candidate by the right hand), and with it the pass, token, token of the pass, grip, and word of a Fellow Craft. As you are yet uninformed, your conductor will answer for you.

The Worshipful Master now takes the candidate by the

*Pass grip of a Fellow Craft*

Entered Apprentice's grip, and says to his conductor, the S.D., while holding the candidate by this grip:

W. M.--Here I left you, and here I find you. Will you be off or from?

S. D. (for candidate) From.

W. M.--From what, and to what?

S. D.--From the real grip of an Entered Apprentice to the pass grip of a Fellow Craft.

W. M.--Pass.

Here the candidate is requested to pass his thumb from the first joint to the space between the first and second joints, which is the pass grip of a Fellow Craft.

W. M.--What is that?

Conductor--The pass grip of a Fellow Craft.

W. M.--Has it a name?

Conductor--It has.

W. M.--Will you give it me?

Conductor--"Shibboleth." (Some letter it, Shib-bo-leth.)

W. M.--Will you be off or from?

*Real grip of a Fellow Craft*

Conductor--From.

W. M.--From what, and to what?

Conductor--From the pass grip of a Fellow Craft to the real grip of the same.

W. M. (moving his thumb to the second joint)--Pass.

W. M.--What is that?

Conductor--The real grip of a Fellow Craft.

W. M.--Has it a name?

Conductor--It has.

W. M.--Will you give it me?

Conductor--I did not so receive it, neither can I so impart it.

W. M.--How will you dispose of it?

Conductor--I will letter it or halve it.

W. M.--Halve it, and begin.

Conductor--No, you begin.

W. M.--Begin you.

Conductor--Ja. [pronounced "Ya"]

W. M.--Chin.

Conductor--Jachin. ["Yachin"]

W. M.--The pass is right. (At the words, "is right," lifting candidate from his knees at the altar.) You will arise, and salute the Junior and Senior Wardens as a Fellow Craft.

The conductor having previously removed the cable-tow from the candidate's arm, he conducts him to the Junior Warden's station in the south, halts before that officer, and gives two raps on the floor with his rod, or stamps twice on the floor with his foot, which is responded to by the Junior Warden, in like manner, with his gavel.

[...]

W. M.--Brother Senior Deacon, you will reconduct the candidate to the Senior Warden in the west, with my orders that he teach him how to wear his apron as a Fellow Craft.

It should be here remarked that when a candidate is prepared in the ante-room for the Fellow Craft's degree, he has an apron tied on him, with the flap up, as worn by an Entered Apprentice, which he wears until he arrives at this part of the ceremony.

The Deacon now conducts the candidate to the Senior Warden's station. This officer leaves his seat, and, approaching candidate, turns the flap of his apron down, at the same time saying--Brother, at the building of King Solomon's Temple, the Fellow Crafts wore their aprons with the flap turned down and the corner turned up, and thus you will wear yours, until further advanced. (Tucks a corner under the string.)

The conductor now reconducts the candidate to the Worshipful Master in the east.

W. M.--I now present you with the working tools of a Fellow Craft Mason, which are the plumb, square, and level.

The Master here shows the candidate these tools, which are generally made of rosewood or ebony, and kept for these occasions on the Master's desk.

W. M.--The Plumb is an instrument made use of by operative masons to raise perpendiculars, the Square to square their work, and the Level to lay horizontals; but we, as Free and Accepted Masons, are taught to make use of them for more noble and glorious purposes; the Plumb admonishes us to walk uprightly in our several stations before God and man, squaring our actions by the Square of Virtue, and remembering that we are traveling upon the Level of Time, to "that undiscovered country, from whose bourne no traveler returns."

W. M.--Brother Senior Deacon, it is my orders that you reconduct this candidate to the place from whence he came (ante-room), and invest him of what he has been divested of, preparatory to making an ascent through a porch, by a flight of winding stairs, consisting of three, five, and seven steps, to a place representing the Middle Chamber of King Solomon's Temple, there to receive instructions relative to the wages and jewels of a Fellow Craft.

The conductor then leads the candidate to the centre of the Lodge, before the altar, and makes the duegard and sign of a Fellow Craft, which is responded to by the Master. They then retire from the Lodge to the ante-room. After the candidate is out of the room, the Lodge is arranged for his second reception and the completion of the Degree. Two large pillars, each from six and a half to seven feet high, are placed near the door, about five feet apart, and fifteen pieces of painted board, of a rectangular form, are arranged upon the carpet so as to represent three, five, and seven steps, or stairs. Some Lodges, especially those in the large cities, employ real steps, but in most country Lodges the painted boards are used.

After the candidate is dressed, the conductor ties upon him a white apron, with the flap turned down, as worn by Fellow Crafts. The conductor then opens the Lodge-door, and, taking the candidate by the left arm, he leads him forward through the door in front of the pillars.

Conductor--Brother Gabe, we are now about to make an ascent through a porch, by a flight of winding stairs, consisting of three, five, and seven steps, to a place representing the Middle Chamber of King Solomon's Temple, there to receive instructions relative to the wages due, and jewels of a Fellow Craft.

[...] Our ancient brethren worked at both Operative and Speculative Masonry; they worked at the building of King Solomon's Temple, besides numerous other Masonic edifices. They wrought six days, but did not work on the seventh, for in six days God created the heavens and the earth, and rested on the seventh day; therefore our ancient brethren consecrated this day as a day of rest from their labors; thereby enjoying frequent opportunities to contemplate the glorious works of creation, and to adore their great Creator.

Brother, the first thing that particularly attracts our attention are (here the conductor steps forward) two large brazen pillars (pointing at them with his rod), one on the right and one on the left hand. The name of the one on the left hand is Boaz, and signifies strength; the name of the one on the right is Jachin, and denotes establishment; they, collectively, denote establishment and strength, and allude to a passage in Scripture: "In strength shall this house be established." These are representations of the two pillars erected at the outer porch of King Solomon's Temple. They are said to have been in height thirty-five cubits, twelve in circumference, and four in diameter; they are said to have been adorned with two large chapiters of five cubits each, making their entire height forty cubits. These chapiters were ornamented with a representation of net-work, lily-work, and pomegranates, and are said to denote Unity, Peace, and Plenty. The network, from its connection, denotes unity; the lily-work, from its whiteness, and the retired place in which it grows, purity and peace; the pomegranates, from the exuberance of their seed, plenty. These chapiters have on the top of each a globe, or ball; these globes are two artificial spherical bodies, on the convex surfaces of which are represented the countries, seas, and various parts of the earth, the face of the heavens, the planetary revolutions, and are said to be thus extensive, to denote the universality of Masonry, and that a Mason's charity ought to be equally extensive. The principal use of these globes, besides serving as maps, to distinguish the outward parts of the earth and the situation of the fixed stars, is to illustrate and explain the phenomena arising from the annual revolution and the diurnal rotation of the earth around its own axis. They are the noblest instruments for improving the mind, and giving it the most distinct idea of any problem or proposition, as well as enabling it to solve the same.

Contemplating these bodies, we are inspired with a due reverence for the Deity and his works and are induced to encourage the studies of astronomy, geography, navigation, and the arts dependent on them, by which society has been so much benefited.

The composition of these pillars is molten or cast brass; they were cast whole, on the banks of the river Jordan, in the clay grounds between SUCCOTH and ZAREDATHA, where King Solomon ordered these and all holy vessels to be cast.

They were cast hollow, and were four inches or a hand's breadth thick. They were cast hollow the better to withstand inundation and conflagrations, and are said to have contained the archives of Masonry.

Conductor--Brother, we will pursue our journey. (Stepping to the three steps on the floor or carpet.) The next thing that attracts our attention are the winding stairs which lead to the Middle Chamber of King Solomon's Temple, consisting of three, five, and seven steps.

The first three allude to the three principal stages of human life, namely, youth, manhood, and old age. In youth, as Entered Apprentices, we ought industriously to occupy our minds in the attainment of useful knowledge; in manhood, as Fellow Crafts, we should apply our knowledge to the discharge of our respective duties to God, our neighbors, and ourselves; so that in old age, as Master Masons, we may enjoy the happy reflections consequent on a well-spent life, and die in the hope of a glorious immortality.

They also allude to the three principal supports in Masonry, namely, Wisdom, Strength, and Beauty; for it is necessary that there should be wisdom to contrive, strength to support, and beauty to adorn all great and important undertakings.

They further allude to the three principal officers of the Lodge, viz.: Master, and Senior and Junior Wardens.

Stepping forward to the five steps, he continues:

The five steps allude to the five orders of architecture and the five human senses.

The five orders of architecture are Tuscan, Doric, Ionic, Corinthian, and Composite. [...]

The five human senses are hearing, seeing, feeling, smelling, and tasting, the first three of which have ever been highly esteemed among Masons: hearing, to hear the word; seeing, to see the sign; feeling, to feel the grip, whereby one Mason may know another in the dark as well as in the light. (Steps forward to the seven steps.)

The seven steps allude to the seven Sabbatical years, seven years of famine, seven years in building the Temple, seven golden candlesticks, seven wonders of the world, seven wise men of the east, seven planets; but, more especially, the seven liberal arts and sciences, which are grammar, rhetoric, logic, arithmetic, geometry, music, and astronomy. For this and many other reasons the number seven has ever been held in high estimation among Masons.

Grammar is the science which teaches us how to express our ideas in appropriate words, which we afterward beautify and adorn with Rhetoric; while Logic instructs us how to think and reason with propriety, and to make language sub-ordinate to thought.

Arithmetic, which is the science of computing by numbers, is absolutely essential, not only to a thorough knowledge of all mathematical science, but also to a proper pursuit of our daily vocations.

Geometry treats of the powers and properties of magnitudes in general, where length, breadth and thickness are considered — from a point to a line, from a line to a superficies, and from a superficies to a solid. A point is the beginning of all geometrical matter. A line is the continuation of the same. A superficies has length and breadth without a given thickness. A solid has length and breadth with a given thickness, which forms a cube and comprehends the whole.

By this science the architect is enabled to construct his plans and execute his designs; the general to arrange his soldiers; the engineer to mark out grounds for encampments; the geographer to give the dimensions of the world and all things therein contained – to delineate the extent of the seas, and specify the divisions of empires, kingdoms and provinces. By it also, the astronomer is enabled to make his observations, and to fix the duration of times and seasons, years and cycles. In fine, Geometry is the foundation of architecture and the root of mathematics.

To be without a perception of the charms of Music is to be without the finer traits of humanity. It is the medium which gives the natural world communication with the spiritual, and few are they who have not felt its power and acknowledged its expressions to be intelligible to the heart. It is a language of delightful sensations, far more eloquent than words. It breathes to the ear the clearest intimations; it touches and gently agitates the agreeable and sublime passions; it wraps us in melancholy and elevates us to joy; it dissolves and inflames; it melts us in tenderness and excites us to war.

[...]

Astronomy is that sublime science which inspires the contemplative mind to soar aloft and read the wisdom, strength and beauty of the Great Creator in the heavens. How nobly eloquent of the Deity is the celestial hemisphere – spangled with the most magnificent heralds of His infinite glory! They speak to the whole universe; for there is no people so barbarous as to fail to understand their language; no nation so distant that their voices are not heard among them.

By this time the Senior Deacon has passed the entire representation of the flight of stairs, and is now at the Junior Warden's station in the south. Upon arriving here, he (the Senior Deacon) says to the candidate:

Brother, we are now approaching the outer door of King Solomon's Temple, which appears to be tyled or guarded by the Junior Warden.

As they approach the Junior Warden's desk, he (the Junior Warden) exclaims:

J. W.--Who comes here?

S. D.--A Craftsman, on his way to the Middle Chamber of King Solomon's Temple.

J. W.--How do you expect to gain admission?

S. D.--By the pass, and token of the pass of a Fellow Craft.

J. W.--Give me the pass.

S. D.--Shibboleth.

J. W.--What does that denote?

S. D.--Plenty.

J. W.--How is it represented?

S. D.--By ears of corn hanging near a water-ford.

J. W.--Why originated this word as a pass?

S. D.--In consequence of a quarrel which long existed between Jephthah, judge of Israel, and the Ephraimites:

the latter had been a stubborn, rebellious people, whom Jephthah had endeavored to subdue by lenient measures, but to no effect. The Ephraimites, being highly incensed for not being called to fight, and share in the rich spoils of the Ammonitish war, assembled a mighty army, and passed over the river Jordan to give Jephthah battle; but he, being apprised of their approach, called together the men of *Gilead*, and gave them battle, and put them to flight; and, to make his victory more complete, he ordered guards to be placed on the different passes on the banks of the river Jordan, and commanded, if the Ephraimites passed that way, Say ye *Shibboleth*; but they, being of a different tribe, could not frame to pronounce it aright, and pronounced it *Sibboleth*; which trifling defect proved them to be spies, and cost them their lives; and there fell at that time, at the different passes on the banks of the river Jordan, forty and two thousand. This word was also used by our ancient brethren to distinguish a friend from a foe, and has since been adopted as a password, to be given before entering every regulated and well-governed Lodge of Fellow Crafts.

J. W.--Give me the token (here give the pass grip of a Fellow Craft, see figure, page 52).

J. W.--The pass is right, and the token is right; pass on.

They now pass around the Junior Warden's station, and go to the Senior Warden's Station in the west, and as they approach the Senior Warden's station the Senior Deacon remarks:

Brother, we are now coming to the inner door of

the Middle Chamber of King Solomon's Temple, which appears to be guarded by the Senior Warden in the west.

S. W.--Who comes here?

S. D.--A Craftsman, on his way to the Middle Chamber.

S. W.--How do you expect to gain admission?

S. D.--By the grip and word of a Fellow Craft.

S. W.--Give me the grip (here give the real grip of a Fellow Craft--see figure, page 53).

S. W.--What is that?

S. D.--The real grip of a Fellow Craft.

S. W.--Has it a name?

S. D.--It has.

S. W.--Will you give it me?

S. D.--I did not so receive it, neither can I so impart it.

S. W.--How will you dispose of it?

S. D.--I will letter it, or halve it with you.

S. W.--Halve it, and begin.

S. D.--No, you begin.

S. W.--Begin you.

S. D.--Ja.

S. W.--Chin.

S. D.--Jachin.

S. W.--The word is right, and the grip is right; pass on, brother.

They pass on to the Worshipful Master in the east, and on their arrival at his desk, the Master rises from his seat, and says:

W. M.--Brother Gabe, you have now arrived at the place representing the Middle Chamber of King Solomon's Temple, where you will be received and recorded as a Fellow Craft.

Turning to the Secretary's desk, he continues.

W. M.--Brother Secretary, you will make the record.

Sec.--It is so recorded.

W. M.--[...] You have now arrived at the Middle Chamber where you are received and recorded a Fellow Craft. You are now entitled to wages, as such; which are, the *Corn* of nourishment, the *Wine* of refreshment, and the *Oil* of joy, which denote peace, harmony, and strength. You are also entitled to the jewels of a Fellow Craft; which are, an attentive ear, an instructive tongue, and faithful breast. The attentive ear receives the sound from the instructive tongue, and the mysteries of Masonry are safely lodged in the repository of faithful breasts.

W. M.--I shall now direct your attention to the letter "G" (here the Master turns and points to a large gilded letter "G," which is generally placed on the wall back of the Master's seat and above his head; some Lodges suspend it in front of the Master, by a cord or wire), which is the initial of geometry, the fifth science, it being that on which this Degree was principally founded.

Geometry, the first and noblest of sciences, is the basis

upon which the superstructure of Masonry is erected. By geometry, we may curiously trace nature through her various windings to her most concealed recesses. By it we discover the power, the wisdom, and the goodness of the Grand Artificer of the Universe, and view with delight the proportions which connect this vast machine. By it we discover how the planets move in their different orbits, and demonstrate their various revolutions. By it we account for the return of the seasons, and the variety of scenes which each season displays to the discerning eye. Numerous worlds are around us, all formed by the same Divine Artist, and which roll through the vast expanse, and are all conducted by the same unerring law of nature. A survey of nature, and the observation of her beautiful proportions, first determined man to imitate the Divine plan, and study symmetry and order. This gave rise to societies, and birth to every useful art. The architect began to design, and the plans which he laid down, being improved by experience and time, have produced works which are the admiration of every age.

The lapse of time, the ruthless hand of ignorance, and the devastations of war have laid waste and destroyed many valuable monuments of antiquity on which the utmost exertions of human genius have been employed. Even the Temple of Solomon, so spacious and magnificent, and constructed by so many celebrated artists, escaped not the unsparing ravages of barbarous force. Freemasonry, notwithstanding, has still survived. Tools and implements of architecture are selected by the fraternity, to imprint on the memory wise and serious truths; and thus, through a succession of ages, are transmitted unimpaired the excellent tenets of our institution.

W. M.--Brother Gabe, this letter has a higher signification; it alludes to the sacred name of Deity (here he gives three raps with his gavel (• • •), when all in the Lodge rise to their feet), to whom we should all, from the youngest Entered Apprentice, who stands in the northeast corner, to the Worshipful Master, who presides in the east, with all sincerity humbly bow (here all bow their heads), with reverence most humbly bow. (Master gives one rap, when all the brethren take their seats again.)

W. M.--Brother Gabe, this ends this degree.

## THE RITUALS REVEALED: MASTER MASON

## Master Mason, or Third Degree

The Third Degree is said to be the height of Ancient Freemasonry, and the most sublime of all the Degrees in Masonry; and when it is conferred, the Lodge is generally well filled with the members of the Lodge and visiting brethren. The traditional account of the death, several burials, and resurrections of one of the craft, Hiram Abiff, the widow's son, as developed in conferring this Degree, is very interesting.

We read in the Bible that Hiram Abiff was one of the head workmen employed at the building of King Solomon's Temple and other ancient writings inform us that he was an arbiter between King Solomon and Hiram, king of Tyre; but his tragic death is nowhere recorded, except in the archives of Freemasonry. Not even the Bible, the writings of Josephus, nor any other writings, however ancient, of which we have any knowledge, furnish any information respecting his death. It is very singular that a man so celebrated as Hiram Abiff, universally acknowledged as the third most distinguished man then living, and, in many respects, the greatest man in the world, should pass from off the stage of action, in the presence of King Solomon, three thousand three hundred grand overseers, and one hundred and fifty thousand workmen, with whom he had spent a number of years, and with King Solomon, his bosom friend, without any of his numerous *confrères* even recording his death, or any thing about it.

A Master Masons' Lodge is styled by the Craft the "Sanctum Sanctorum, or Holy of Holies, of King Solomon's Temple," and when the Lodge is opened on this Degree, both points of the compasses are elevated above the square.

The candidate is divested of all wearing apparel, except his shirt and drawers, and if he has not the latter, he is furnished with a pair by the brethren preparing him. The drawers are rolled up just above the candidate's knees,

*Master Mason duly and truly prepared*

and both arms are taken out of his shirt-sleeves, leaving his legs and breast bare. [A] cable-tow is wound around his body three times, and a bandage, or hoodwink, is tied very closely over his eyes (see figure, above).

When the candidate is prepared, the Deacon takes him by the left arm, leads him up to the door of the Lodge, and gives three *loud, distinct knocks*.

The Senior Deacon, who has stationed himself at the inner door, at the right of the Senior Warden, on hearing these raps rises to his feet, makes the sign of a Master Mason to the Master, and says:

Worshipful Master, while engaged in the lawful pursuit of Masonry, there is an alarm at the inner door of our Lodge.

W. M.--You will attend to the alarm, and ascertain the cause.

Senior Deacon gives three loud knocks (• • •), which are responded to by one (•) from the parties outside. The Senior Deacon then answers with one rap (•), and opens the door.

S. D.--Who comes here?

J. D.--Brother Gabe, who has been regularly initiated Entered Apprentice, passed to the Degree of Fellow Craft, and now wishes to receive further light in Masonry, by being raised to the sublime Degree of a Master Mason.

S. D.--Brother Gabe, is it of your own free-will and accord?

Candidate--It is.

S. D.--Brother Junior Deacon, is he worthy and well qualified?

J. D.--He is.

S. D.--Duly and truly prepared?

J. D--He is.

S. D.--Has he made suitable proficiency in the preceding degrees?

J. D.--He has.

S. D.--And properly vouched for?

J. D.--He is.

S. D.--Who vouches for him?

J. D.--A brother.

S. D.--By what further right or benefit does he expect to gain admission?

J. D.--By the benefit of the password.

S. D.--Has he the password?

J. D.--He has it not, but I have it for him.

S. D.--Advance, and give it me.

Junior Deacon here steps forward and whispers in the Senior Deacon's ear, "Tubal Cain."

S. D.--The pass is right; you will wait with patience until the Worshipful Master is informed of your request and his answer returned.

The Deacon then closes the door, repairs to the centre of the Lodge-room before the altar, and sounds his rod on the floor three times (• • •), which is responded to by the Master with three raps of the gavel. [...]

S. D.--Brother Gabe, on entering this Lodge the first time, you were received on the point of the compasses, pressing your naked left breast, the moral of which was explained to you. On entering the second time, you were received on the angle of the square, which was also explained to you. I now receive you on both points of the compasses, extending from your naked left to your naked right breast (he here places both points against candidate's breasts), which is to teach you, that as the vital parts of man are contained within the breasts, so the most excellent tenets of our institution are contained between the points of the compasses-- which are Friendship, Morality, and Brotherly Love. [...]

W. M.--From whence came you, and whither are you traveling?

S. D.--From the west, traveling toward the east.

W. M.--Why leave you the west, and travel toward the east?

S. D--In search of further light in Masonry.

W. M.--Since that is the object of your search, you will reconduct this candidate to the Senior Warden in the west, with my orders that he be taught to approach the east, the place of further light in Masonry, by three upright, regular steps, his body erect at the altar before the Worshipful Master in the east.

The Senior Deacon then conducts the candidate to the Senior Warden in the west, and reports:

S. D.--Brother Senior Warden, it is the orders of the Worshipful Master that you teach this candidate to approach the east, the place of further light in Masonry, by three upright, regular steps, his body erect at the altar before the Worshipful Master in the east.

The Senior Warden approaches the candidate, faces him towards the east (i.e. towards the Master), and says:

Brother, you will step off with your left foot one full step, and bring the heel of your right in the hollow of your left foot; now step off with your right foot, and bring the heel of your left in the hollow of your right foot; now step off with your left foot, and bring both heels together.

S. W.--The candidate is in order, Worshipful, and awaits your further will and pleasure.

W. M.--You will cause him to kneel on his naked knees, both hands resting on the Holy Bible, square, and compasses.

W. M.--Brother Gabe, you are kneeling, for the third time, at the altar of Masonry, to take upon yourself the solemn oath of a Master Mason; and I, as Master of this Lodge, take pleasure, as on former occasions, in informing you that there is nothing in it which will interfere with the duty you owe to your God, your neighbor, your country, or self. Are you willing to take the oath?

Candidate--I am.

W. M.--You will repeat your name, and say after me:

[The oath is the same as for the two previous degrees, with the following additions]:

"I furthermore promise and swear that I will stand to and abide by all laws, rules, and regulations of the Master Masons' Degree, and of the Lodge of which I may here-after become a member, as far as the same shall come to my knowledge; and that I will ever maintain and support the constitution, laws, and edicts of the Grand Lodge under which the same shall be holden.

"Further, that I will acknowledge and obey all due signs and summonses sent to me from a Master Masons' Lodge, or given me by a brother of that Degree, if within the length of my cable-tow.

"Further, that I will always aid and assist all poor, distressed, worthy Master Masons, their widows and orphans, knowing them to be such, as far as their necessities may require, and my ability permit, without material injury to myself and family.

"Further, that I will keep a worthy brother Master

Mason's secrets inviolable, when communicated to and received by me as such, murder and treason excepted.

"Further, that I will not aid, nor be present at, the initiation, passing, or raising of a woman, an old man in his dotage, a young man in his nonage, an atheist, a madman, or fool, knowing them to be such.

"Further, that I will not sit in a Lodge of clandestine-made Masons, nor converse on the subject of Masonry with a clandestine-made Mason, nor one who has been expelled or suspended from a Lodge, while under that sentence, knowing him or them to be such.

"Further, I will not cheat, wrong, nor defraud a Master Mason's Lodge, nor a brother of this Degree knowingly, nor supplant him in any of his laudable undertakings, but will give him due and timely notice, that he may ward off all danger.

"Further, that I will not knowingly strike a brother Master Mason, or otherwise do him personal violence in anger, except in the necessary defence of my family or property.

"Further, that I will not have illegal carnal intercourse with a Master Mason's wife, his mother, sister, or daughter, nor suffer the same to be done by others, if in my power to prevent.

"Further, that I will not give the Grand Masonic word, in any other manner or form than that in which I shall receive it, and then in a low breath.

"Further, that I will not give the Grand Hailing Sign of Distress, except in case of the most imminent danger, in a just and lawful Lodge, or for the benefit of instruction; and if ever I should see it given, or hear the words accompanying it, by a worthy brother in distress, I will fly to his relief, if there is a greater probability of saving his life than losing my own.

"All this I most solemnly, sincerely promise and swear, with a firm and steady resolution to perform the same, without any hesitation, mental reservation, or secret evasion of mind what-ever, binding myself, under no less penalty than that of having my body severed in two, my bowels taken from thence and burned to ashes, the ashes scattered before the four winds of heaven, that no more remembrance might be had of so vile and wicked a wretch as I would be, should I ever, knowingly, violate this my Master Mason's obligation. So help me God, and keep me steadfast in the due performance of the same."

W. M.--You will detach your hands and kiss the book. In your present condition, what do you most desire?

Candidate (prompted by conductor)--Further light in Masonry.

W. M.--Let him receive further light.

Conductor here takes off the hoodwink and removes the cable-tow, and all around the altar place their hands in the position of the duegard of a Master Mason. The Worshipful Master gives one rap with his gavel, when all the brethren retire to their seats, leaving at the altar the Master, conductor, and candidate.

W. M.--Brother Gabe, on receiving further light, you perceive more than you have heretofore. Both points of the compasses are elevated above the square, which is to teach you never to lose sight of those truly Masonic virtues, which are friendship, morality, and brotherly love.

The Master now steps back about three paces from the altar, and says:

Brother Gabe, you discover me approaching you from the east, under the duegard of a Master Mason; and, in token of the further continuance of my brotherly love and favor, I present you with my right hand, and with it the pass and token of the pass of a Master Mason.

Takes the candidate by the "real grip" of a Fellow Craft, and says:

Your conductor will answer for you.

W. M.--Will you be off or from?

Conductor--From.

W. M.--From what and to what?

Conductor--From the "real grip" of a Fellow Craft to the pass grip of a Master Mason.

W. M.--Pass.

Conductor here instructs candidate to pass his thumb from the second joint to space beyond, which is the second space.

W. M. (looking conductor in the eye)--What is that?

*Pass grip of a Master Mason*

Conductor--The pass grip of a Master Mason.

W. M.--Has it a name?

Conductor--It has.

W. M.--Will you give it me?

Conductor--I did not so receive it, neither can I so impart it.

W. M.--How will you dispose of it?

Conductor--I will letter it or halve it.

W. M.--Halve it, and begin.

Conductor--No, you begin.

W. M.--Begin you.

Conductor--Tu.

W. M.--Bal.

Conductor--Cain. (Pronounced by the conductor--Tubal Cain.)

W. M. (lifting the candidate up)--You will arise, and salute the Junior and Senior Wardens as an obligated Master Mason. [...]

The conductor then turns about to the Senior Warden in the west, and says:

Brother Senior Warden, it is the orders of the Worshipful Master that you teach this candidate how to wear his apron as a Master Mason.

The Senior Warden approaches the candidate and ties the apron upon him, with the flap and corners turned down, and says:

Master Masons wear their aprons with the flap and corners down, to designate them as Master Masons, or as overseers of the work, and so you will wear yours.

The conductor now conducts the candidate back to the Worshipful Master in the east.

W. M.--Brother Gabe, as you are clothed as a Master Mason, it is necessary that you should have the working-tools of a Master Mason. (Master has a small trowel, which he shows the candidate as he commences to read concerning it.)

The working-tools of a Master Mason are all the implements of Masonry appertaining to the first three degrees indiscriminately, but more especially the trowel.

The trowel is an instrument made use of by operative masons to spread the cement which unites a building into one common mass; but we, as Free and Accepted Masons are taught to make use of it for the more noble and glorious purpose of spreading the cement of brotherly love and affection; that cement which unites us into one sacred band, or society of friends and brothers, among whom no contention should ever exist, but that noble contention, or rather emulation, of who best can work and best agree. [...]

The room is cleared by removing the altar and lights, and the two large pillars used in the Second Degree. By this time the candidate is dressed, his apron is tied on as a Master Mason, with the right-hand corner tucked up, and he wears a yoke with a Senior Warden's jewel attached to it. In some Lodges, the brethren on this occasion attire the candidate with a very rich apron and yoke.

When the candidate is fully dressed, the door is unceremoniously thrown open, and he, in company with others, is permitted to enter the Lodge. His friends now approach him, and congratulate him upon his Masonic appearance, asking him how he likes the degree, and if he is not glad he is through, &c., &c.

The object of this is to mislead the candidate, and to impress upon his mind the idea that there is no more of the ceremony, and that his initiation is completed. [...]

After the candidate is conducted to the east, before the Master, the conductor takes his position behind the candidate, with a hoodwink either in his hand or secreted in his pocket.

W. M. (looking candidate seriously in the face)--Brother Gabe, I presume you now consider yourself a Master Mason, and, as such, entitled to all the privileges of a Master Mason, do you not?

Candidate--I do.

W. M.--I presumed that you did from the jewel that you wear, it being the Senior Warden's jewel.

W. M.--Brother Gabe, you are not yet a Master Mason, neither do I know that you ever will be, until I know how well you will withstand the amazing trials and dangers that await you. The Wardens and brethren of this Lodge require a more satisfactory proof of your fidelity to your trust, before they are willing to intrust you with the more valuable secrets of this Degree. You have a rough and rugged road to travel, beset with thieves, robbers, and murderers; and should you lose your life in the attempt, it will not be the first instance of the kind, my brother. You will remember in whom you put your trust, with that divine assurance, that "he who endureth unto the end, the same shall be saved." Heretofore you have had some one to pray for you, but now you have none. You must pray for yourself. You will therefore suffer yourself to be again hoodwinked, and kneel where you are, and pray orally or mentally, as you please. When through, signify by saying Amen, and arise and pursue your journey.

The candidate then kneels, and the conductor ties a hoodwink very closely over both eyes, so that he cannot see.

After the candidate has said Amen, and the Lodge-room has been darkened by turning down the gaslights or lamps, the conductor takes the candidate by the right arm, assists him to arise, and they proceed to travel three times around the room, traveling with the sun. As they start, the conductor commences to relate to the candidate the following:

Conductor--Brother, it was the usual custom of our Grand Master, Hiram Abiff (this is the first he hears about Hiram Abiff), to enter into the unfinished "Sanctum Sanctorum," or "Holy of Holies" of King Solomon's Temple, each day at high twelve, while the craft were called from labor to refreshment, for the purpose of drawing out his designs upon the trestle-board, whereby the craft might pursue their labors; after which, it was further his custom to offer up his devotions to the Deity. Then he would retire at the south gate of the outer courts of the Temple; and, in conformity with the custom of our Grand Master, whose memory we all so reverently adore, we will now retire at the south gate of the Temple.

They have now passed around the Lodge three times, and as they approach the Junior Warden's station in the south, he steps silently out from his seat to the floor, and confronts the blind-folded candidate, clinching him by the collar in a very rough manner, and at the same time exclaiming:

J. W. (Jubela, First Ruffian)--Grand Master Hiram, I am glad to meet you thus alone. I have long sought this opportunity. You will remember you promised us that when the Temple was completed, we should receive the secrets of a Master Mason, whereby we might travel in foreign countries, work, and receive Master's wages. Behold! The

Temple is now about to be completed, and we have not obtained that which we have so long sought. At first, I did not doubt your veracity; but now I do! (Gives candidate a sudden twitch by the collar.) I therefore now demand of you the secrets of a Master Mason!

Conductor (for candidate)--Brother, this is an unusual way of asking for them. It is neither a proper time nor place; but be true to your engagement, and I will be true to mine. Wait until the Temple is completed, and then, if you are found worthy and well qualified, you will unquestionably receive the secrets of a Master Mason; but, until then, you cannot.

Ruffian--This (shaking candidate) does not satisfy me! Talk not to me of time or place, but give me the secrets of a Master Mason, or I will take your life!

Conductor--I cannot; nor can they be given, except in the presence of Solomon, king of Israel, Hiram, king of Tyre, and myself.

Ruffian--That does not satisfy me. I'll hear no more of your cavilling! (Clinches candidate more fiercely.) Give me the Master's word, or I will take your life in a moment!

Conductor--I shall not!

The Ruffian gives the candidate a brush across the throat with his right hand, and at the same time relinquishes his hold with his left, steps quietly to one side, and permits the conductor and candidate to pass on to the Senior Warden's station in the west, which is done by the conductor advancing very rapidly, pulling the candidate along with him. As they approach the west, the Senior Warden steps out as did the Junior Warden, facing the candidate, and, clinching him by the collar more roughly than the Junior Warden, exclaiming as follows:

S. W. (Second Ruffian)--Give me the secrets of a Master Mason!

Conductor (for candidate)--I cannot.

Ruffian--Give me the secrets of a Master Mason! (Shakes candidate.)

Conductor--I shall not.

Ruffian--Give me the Master's word, or I will take your life in a moment! (Gives candidate a sudden shake.)

Conductor--I will not!

Ruffian gives candidate a brush with his right hand across the left breast, and at the same time lets him pass, the conductor hurrying him on towards the east end of the Lodge, where the Master is stationed to perform the part of the Third Ruffian, Jubelum, who is generally provided with a buckskin bag stuffed with hair, to represent a setting-maul.

As the candidate is hurried along towards Jubelum (Worshipful Master), the latter seizes him with both hands by the collar of his coat, and swings him round, so as to place his back towards the east, with his heels a few inches from the edge of the canvas before alluded to. This canvas is usually held behind the candidate, in an inclined position, by some of the brethren, and is for the purpose of catching him when he is tripped up by the assumed ruffian, Jubelum. The Master (Third Ruffian) then exclaims:

W. M. (as Third Ruffian)--Give me the secrets of a Master Mason!

Conductor (for candidate)--I cannot!

Ruffian--Give me the secrets of a Master Mason, or I will take your life!

Conductor--I shall not!

Ruffian--You have (here Master seizes the candidate more fiercely, and affects a great earnestness of purpose) escaped "Jubela" and "Jubelo"; me you cannot escape; my name is "Jubelum!" What I purpose, that I perform. I hold in my hand an instrument of death; therefore, give me the Master's word, or I will take your life in a moment!

Conductor--I will not!

Ruffian--Then die!

The Worshipful Master here gives the candidate a blow on his head with a buckskin bag, or setting-maul; at the same time, pushing him backward, brings the candidate's heels against the edge of the canvas, trips him up, and the candidate falls upon his back, caught in the canvas clear of the floor, unharmed, but, in many instances, badly frightened.

[...] As the candidate falls into the canvas the brethren lower it to the floor, when the following dialogue ensues

*Third Ruffian, Jubelum, at left, generally the W. M. in the east.*
*Members of the Lodge, in the act of holding the canvas to catch the*
*candidate*

between those who held the canvas and the Master, or the brother acting as the Third Ruffian.

Ruffian--Is he dead?

Answer--He is, his skull is broken in.

Ruffian--What horrid deed is this we have done?

Answer--We have murdered our Grand Master, Hiram Abiff, and have not obtained that which we have sought: this is no time for vain reflection--the question is, what shall we do with the body?

Answer--We will bury it in the rubbish of the Temple, until low twelve, and then we will meet and give it a decent burial.

Answer--Agreed! [...]

A sufficient number of the brethren now take up the body (yet rolled up in the canvas), and, raising it on their shoulders, proceed to carry it around the Lodge, head foremost, three times, in representation of ascending a hill, the last time halting in the west end of the Lodge, nearly in front of the Senior Warden's station, and a little to the right. Upon arriving there they commence to lower it into the grave, as they style it, but in reality only from their shoulders to the floor. After the candidate is lowered, one of the ruffians says:

Let us plant an acacia at the head of the grave, in order to conceal it so that the place may be known should occasion hereafter require.

Some Lodges have a small box with a house-plant or dry twig in it, which is set down on the floor near the candidate's head. [...]

They now retire from the body, in different directions. When all has been again quiet in the Lodge for a few seconds, the brethren jump up, commence laughing, singing, &c., exclaiming:

No work to-day. Craftsmen, we are having good times; I wonder if it will last.

They shuffle about a few moments, when they are called to order by the sound of the gavel from the Master's seat in the east, who inquires in a loud voice as follows:

W. M. (now styled King Solomon)--Brother Junior Grand Warden, what means all this confusion among the workmen? Why are they not at work as usual?

S. W. (now styled J. G. W.)--Most Worshipful King Solomon, there is no work laid out for us, and it is said we can have none. No designs are drawn on the trestle-board, and for this reason many of us are idle.

K. S.--No work laid out--no designs drawn on the trestle-board? What is the meaning of this? Where is our Grand Master, Hiram Abiff?

J. G. W.--We do not know, Most Worshipful King Solomon. He has not been seen since high twelve yesterday.

K. S.--Not been seen since high twelve yesterday! I fear he is indisposed. It is my orders that strict search be made for him through the apartments of the Temple, and due inquiry made. Let him be found, if possible.

[A great search is made all around the lodge for Hiram Abiff] [...]

By this time they have got near the candidate (who is still lying on the floor, rolled up in the canvas), when one of the party sits down near his head, and at the same time says:

"Well, brothers, I am very weary; I must sit down and rest before I can go any farther."

One of his companions exclaims: "I am tired, too!" and sits down near the candidate.

[...] One of the brethren then replies: "We will go a southwesterly course, and will come up with our broth-ers." Attempting to get up, he exclaims, "Hallo! what's this?", at the same time pulling up the evergreen--or acacia, as it is styled--at the head of the grave. "What means this acacia coming up so easily? The ground has been newly broken; this has the appearance of a grave," pointing to the candidate on the floor.

One of the brothers, representing one of the three ruffians, in a corner near by, is now heard to exclaim, in a loud, but deep tone of voice:

"Oh! that my throat had been cut across, my tongue torn out by its roots, and buried in the rough sands of the sea, at low-water mark, where the tide ebbs and flows twice in twenty-four hours, ere I had been accessory to the death of so good a man as our Grand Master, Hiram Abiff."

"Hark! that is the voice of Jubela."

"Oh! that my breast had been torn open, my heart plucked out, and placed upon the highest pinnacle of the Temple, there to be devoured by the vultures of the air, ere I had consented to the death of so good a man as our Grand Master, Hiram Abiff."

"Hark! that is the voice of Jubelo."

"Oh! that my body had been severed in two, my bowels taken from thence and burned to ashes, the ashes scattered to the four winds of heaven, that no more remembrance might be had of so vile and wicked a wretch as I. Ah! Jubela, Jubelo, it was I that struck him harder than you both: it was I that gave him the fatal blow; it was I that killed him."

"That is the voice of Jubelum."

The three craftsmen, having stood by the candidate all this time, listening to the ruffians, whose voices they recognize, say one to another:

"What shall we do? There are three of them, and only three of us."

One says:

"Our cause is just; let us rush in and seize them." [...]

They all pass out of the Lodge with a rush, into the ante-room, where they form into a circle. One, acting as the principal mover, raises his right foot from the floor, at the same time his hands, in the manner of slapping them together, makes two false motions, but at the third all bring down their right feet and hands together, producing a very sharp noise. A momentary silence then ensues, during which one of the party groans, as if nearly dying. This is all intended to produce its effect upon the ears of the candidate. It also represents the execution and dying groans of Jubela, the first ruffian, and is repeated twice more to represent the death of the other two ruffians. Some Lodges use a large drum, others roll a large cannon-ball across the ante-room floor, letting it strike on a cushion placed against the wall. This is not, however, practised in city Lodges.

The ruffians being executed, the brethren all return quietly to the Lodge, when one of them reports, in a loud tone of voice:

"Most Worshipful King Solomon, your orders have been duly executed upon the three murderers of Grand Master, Hiram Abiff."

K. S.--You twelve Fellow Crafts will go in search of the body, and, if found, observe whether the Master's word, or a key to it, or any thing that appertains to the Master's Degree, is on or about it.

The brethren representing the twelve repentant conspirators now walk out near the spot where the candidate is lying, and, when close to him, one of the party says:

"Well, brothers, can we find where the acacia was pulled up?"

Approaching the candidate, another replies:

"Yes, this is the place; let us remove the rubbish and dig down here."

A third, lifting up the canvas, says:

"Yes, here is the body of our Grand Master, Hiram Abiff, in a mangled and putrid state. Let us go and report. But what were our orders? We were ordered to observe whether the Master's word, or a key to it, or any thing appertaining to the Master's Degree, was on or about the body; but, brothers, we are only Fellow Crafts, and know nothing about the Master's word, or a key to it, or any thing appertaining to the Master's Degree; we must, however, make an examination, or we will be put to death." […]

All now form in a circle around the body, the Master and Wardens at the head, when the Master makes the sign of "distress" of a Master Mason, which is done by raising both hands and arms above the head (see Grand Hailing Sign of Distress, opposite).

As the Master makes this sign, he says:

"O Lord my God, I fear the Master's word is forever lost!"

*Grand Hailing Sign of Distress*

After the sign is made, the whole party commence marching around the body with the sun, singing the following dirge; and, if the Lodge has an organ or melodeon, it is played on this occasion, in a very solemn and impressive manner.

I
"Solemn strikes the funeral chime,
Notes of our departing time;
As we journey here below,
Through a pilgrimage of woe!"

II
"Mortals, now indulge a tear,
For Mortality is here:
See how wide her trophies wave
O'er the slumbers of the grave!"

III
"Here another guest we bring.
Seraphs of celestial wing,
To our funeral altar come:
Waft this friend and brother home."

IV
"Lord of all! below--above--
Fill our hearts with truth and love;
When dissolves our earthly tie,
Take us to thy Lodge on High."

Master (as K. S.) makes the "grand hailing sign of distress" (Masters make this sign twice), accompanied by the following exclamation: "O Lord my God, I fear the Master's word is forever lost!" [...]

K. S.--O Lord my God! O Lord my God!! O Lord my God!!! Is there no hope for the widow's son? [...]

"My worthy brother of Tyre, what shall we do?"

S. W.--Let us pray.

The brethren now all kneel around the body on one knee. The Master kneels at the head of the candidate, and, taking off his hat, repeats the following prayer:

Thou, O God! knowest our down-sitting and our uprising, and understandest our thoughts afar off. Shield and defend us from the evil intentions of our enemies, and support us under the trials and afflictions we are destined to endure, while traveling through this vale of tears.

Man that is born of a woman is of few days and full of trouble. He cometh forth as a flower, and is cut down: he fleeth also as a shadow, and continueth not. Seeing his days are determined, the number of his months are with thee; thou hast appointed his bounds that he cannot pass; turn from him that he may rest, till he shall accomplish his day. For there is hope of a tree, if it be cut down, that it will sprout again, and that the tender branch thereof will not cease. But man dieth and wasteth away; yea, man giveth up the ghost, and where is he? As the waters fail from the sea, and the flood decayeth and drieth up, so man lieth down, and riseth not up till the heavens shall be no more. Yet, O Lord! have compassion on the children of thy creation, administer them comfort in time of trouble, and save them with an everlasting salvation. Amen.

Response--So mote it be.

All the brethren now rise to their feet.

K. S. (to the S. W.)--My worthy brother of Tyre, I shall endeavor (with your assistance) to raise the body by the strong grip, or lion's paw, of the tribe of Judah (see figure, on following page).

The Master steps to the feet of the candidate, bending over, takes him by the real grip of a Master Mason, places his right foot against the candidate's right foot, and his hand to his back, and, with the assistance of the brethren, raises him up perpendicularly in a standing position, and, when fairly on his feet, gives him the grand

*Real grip of a Master Mason*

Masonic word on the five points of fellowship (see figure, opposite). In the mean time, the canvas is slipped out of the Lodge, and as the Master commences to give or whisper the word in the candidate's ear, some one of the brethren slips off the hoodwink, and this is the first time he has seen light, probably, in an hour. The following is the representation of the Master giving the candidate the grand Masonic word, or at least this is a substitute, for, according to Masonic tradition, the right one was lost at the death of Hiram Abiff. This word cannot be given in any other way, and by Masons is considered a test of all book Masons.

The Master having given the word, which is MAH-HAH-BONE, in low breath, requests the candidate to repeat it with him, which is in this wise:

Master whispers in candidate's ear--Mah.

Candidate--Hah.

Master--Bone.

[…] The Master, stepping back one pace, now says:

"Brother Gabe, you have now received that grand Masonic word, which you have solemnly sworn never to

*Master giving the Grand Masonic Word on the
Five Points of Fellowship*

give in any other way or form than that in which you have received it, which is on the five points of fellowship, and then in low breath.

"The five points of fellowship are--foot to foot, knee to knee, breast to breast, hand to back, and cheek to cheek, or mouth to ear.

"It is done by putting the inside of your right foot to the inside of the right foot of the one to whom you are going to give the word, the inside of your own knee to his, laying your breast close against his, your left hands on each other's back, and each one putting his mouth to the other's right ear.

"1st. Foot to foot--that you will never hesitate to go on foot, and out of your way, to assist and serve a worthy brother.

"2nd. Knee to knee--that you will ever remember a

brother's welfare, as well as your own, in all your adorations to Deity.

"3rd. Breast to breast--that you will ever keep in your breast a brother's secrets, when communicated to and received by you as such, murder and treason excepted.

"4th. Hand to back--that you will ever be ready to stretch forth your hand to assist and save a fallen brother; and that you will vindicate his character behind his back, as well as before his face.

"5th. Cheek to cheek, or mouth to ear--that you will ever caution and whisper good counsel in the ear of an erring brother, and, in the most friendly manner, remind him of his errors, and aid his reformation, giving him due and timely notice, that he may ward off approaching danger." [...]

Brother, be ever mindful of that great change, when we shall be called from labors on earth to that everlasting refreshment in the paradise of God.

Let me admonish you, in the most serious manner, in reference to the close of life, that, when the cold winter of death shall have passed, and the bright summer morn of the resurrection appears, the Sun of Righteousness shall descend and send forth His angels to collect our ransomed dead; then, if we are found worthy, by the benefit of his "pass" we shall gain a ready admission into that celestial Lodge above, where the Supreme Architect of the Universe presides, where we shall see the King in the beauty of holiness, and with him enter into an endless eternity.

# ♦ CHAPTER II ♦

# History and Myth

asonic tradition holds that Freemasonry is as old as Adam, and the following document, *The Constitutions of the Free-Masons* (1734), begins with an account of the mythical history of the movement. It was written by none other than Benjamin Franklin (1706–90), one of the Founding Fathers of America, who was also a confirmed Freemason, rising to the rank of Grand Master of the Pennsylvania Lodge in 1734. Franklin based his *Constitutions* on an earlier document by an English Mason, James Anderson, but only acknowledged this in a note at the end of the document. The *Constitutions* was the first Masonic document to be printed in America – which stands to reason, given Franklin's profession as owner of a printing press. The *Constitutions* has been reprinted in various editions since first publication in 1723, but Masons still abide by the fundamental rules of this book of law today. The sections from Franklin's 1734 version of the Constitutions that follow discuss Masonic history and how a Mason should behave.

# THE
# CONSTITUTIONS
## OF THE
# *FREE-MASONS.*
### CONTAINING THE

*History, Charges, Regulations,* &c. of that most Ancient and Right Worshipful FRATERNITY.

For the Use of the LODGES.

*LONDON* Printed; *Anno* 5723.
Re-printed in *Philadelphia* by special Order, for the Use of the Brethren in *NORTH-AMERICA.*
In the Year of Masonry 5734. *Anno Domini* 1734.

The
CONSTITUTION,
History, Laws, Charges, Orders,
Regulations, and Usages,
of the
Right Worshipful FRATERNITY
OF ACCEPTED
Free-Masons;
Collected from their general RECORDS, and
their faithful TRADITIONS of many Ages.

TO BE READ
*At the Admission of a NEW BROTHER, when
the Master or Warden shall begin, or order some other
Brother to be read as follows:*

*Adam*, our first Parent, created after the Image of God, *the great Architect of the Universe*, must have had the Liberal Sciences, particularly *Geometry*, written on his Heart; for even since the Fall, we find the Principles of it in the Hearts of his Offspring, and which, in process of time, have been drawn forth into a convenient Method of *Proposition*, by observing the Laws of *Proportion* taken from *Mechanism*: So that as the *Mechanical Arts* gave Occasion to the Learned to reduce the Elements of *Geometry* into Method, this noble Science thus reduc'd, is the Foundation of all those Arts (particularly of *Masonry* and *Architecture*), and the Rule by which they are conducted and perform'd.

No doubt *Adam* taught his Sons *Geometry*, and the use of it, in the several *Arts* and *Crafts* convenient, at least for those early Times; for CAIN, we find, built a City, which he call'd CONSECRATED, or DEDICATED, after the Name of his eldest Son ENOCH; and becoming the Prince of the one Half of Mankind, his Posterity would imitate his royal Example in improving both the noble Science and the useful Art.

Nor can we suppose that SETH was less instructed, who being the Prince of the other Half of Mankind, and also the prime Cultivator of *Astronomy*, would take equal care to teach *Geometry* and *Masonry* to his Offspring, who had also the mighty Advantage of *Adam's* living among them.

But without regarding uncertain Accounts, we may safely conclude the *old World*, that lasted 1656 Years, could not be ignorant of *Masonry* ; and that both the Families of *Seth* and *Cain* erected many curious Works, until at length NOAH, the ninth from Seth, was commanded and directed of God to build the *great Ark*, which, tho' of Wood, was certainly fabricated by *Geometry*, and according to the Rules of *Masonry*.

NOAH, and his three Sons, JAPHET, SHEM, and HAM, all *Masons true*, brought with them over the *Flood* the Traditions and Arts of the *Ante-deluvians,* and amply communicated them to their growing Offspring; for about 101 Years after the *Flood* we find a vast Number of 'em, if not the whole Race of *Noah*, in the Vale of *Shinar*, employ'd in building a *City* and large *Tower*, in order to make to them selves a Name, and to prevent their Dispersion. And tho' they carry'd on the Work to a monstrous Height, and by their Vanity provok'd God to confound their Devices, by confounding their Speech, which occasion'd their Dispersion; yet their Skill in *Masonry* is not the less to be celebrated, having spent above 53 Years in that prodigious Work, and upon their Dispersion carry'd the mighty Knowledge with them into distant Parts, where they found the good Use of it in the Settlement of their *Kingdoms, Commonwealths,* and *Dynasties.* [...]

And, no doubt, the Royal Art was brought down to *Egypt* by MITZRAIM, the second Son of *Ham,* about six Years after the Confusion at *Babel,* and after the *Flood* 160 Years, when he led thither his Colony; (for *Egypt* is *Mitzraim* in *Hebrew*) because we find the River *Nile's* overflowing its Banks, soon caus'd an Improvement in *Geometry,* which consequently brought *Masonry* much in request: For the ancient noble Cities, with the other magnificent Edifices of that Country, and particularly the *famous* PYRAMIDS, demonstrate the early Taste and Genius of that ancient Kingdom. Nay, one of those *Egyptian* PYRAMIDS is reckon'd the *First* of the *Seven Wonders* of the World, the Account of which, by Historians and Travellers, is almost incredible. [...]

ABRAM, after the Confusion at *Babel* about 268 Years, was called out of *Ur* of the *Chaldees,* where he learned *Geometry,* and the *Arts* that are perform'd by it, which he would carefully transmit to *Ishmael,* to *Isaac,* and to his Sons by *Keturah;* and by *Isaac,* to *Esau,* and *Jacob,* and the twelve *Patriarchs:* Nay, the *Jews* believe that ABRAM also instructed the *Egyptians* in the *Assyrian* Learning.

[…] And while marching to *Canaan* thro' *Arabia*, under *Moses*, God was pleased to inspire BEZALEEL, of the Tribe of *Judah*, and AHOLIAB, of the Tribe of *Dan*, with Wisdom of Heart for erecting that most glorious Tent, or *Tabernacle*, wherein the *SHECHINAH* resided; which, tho' not of Stone or Brick, was framed, by *Geometry*, a most beautiful Piece of Architecture, (and prov'd afterwards the Model of *Solomon*'s Temple) according to the Pattern that God had shewn to MOSES in the Mount; who therefore became the GENERAL MASTER-MASON, as well as King of *Jessurun*, being well skill'd in all the *Egyptian* Learning, and divinely inspir'd with more sublime Knowledge in *Masonry*.

So that the *Israelites*, at their leaving *Egypt*, were a whole Kingdom of *Masons*, well instructed, under the Conduct of their GRAND MASTER MOSES, who often marshall'd them into a regular and *general Lodge*, while in the Wilderness, and gave them wise *Charges, Orders, &c*. had they been well observ'd! But no more of the Premises must be mention'd.

And after they were possess'd of *Canaan*, the *Israelites* came not short of the old Inhabitants in *Masonry*, but rather vastly improv'd it, by the special Direction of Heaven; they fortify'd better, and improv'd their City-Houses and the Palaces of their Chiefs, and only fell short in *sacred Architecture* while the *Tabernacle* stood, but no longer; for the finest sacred Building of the *Canaanites* was the *Temple* of *Dagon* in *Gaza* of the *Philistines*, very magnificent, and capacious enough to receive 5000 People under its Roof, that was artfully supported by two *main Columns*; and was a wonderful Discovery of their mighty Skill in true Masonry, as must he own'd.

But *Dagon*'s Temple, and the finest Structures of *Tyre* and *Sidon*, could not be compared with the ETERNAL God's Temple at *Jerusalem*, begun and finish'd, to the Amazement of all the World, in the short space of *seven Years* and *six Months*, by that wisest Man and most glorious King of *Israel*, the *Prince of Peace and Architecture*, SOLOMON (the Son of *David*, who was refused that Honour for being a Man of Blood) by divine Direction, without the Noise of Work-mens Tools, though there were employ'd about it no less than 3600 *Princes*, or *Master-Masons*, to conduct the Work according to *Solomon*'s Directions, with 80,000 *Hewers of Stone* in the Mountain, or *Fellow Craftsmen*, and 70,000 *Labourers*, in all − 153,600, besides the Levy under *Adoniram*, to work in the Mountains of *Lebanon* by turns with the *Sidonians*, viz. 30,000 − being in all −183,600, for which great Number of ingenious Masons, *Solomon* was much oblig'd to HIRAM, or *Huram*, King of *Tyre*, who sent his Masons and Carpenters to *Jerusalem*, and the Firs and Cedars of *Lebanon* to *Joppa* the next Sea-port. But above all, he sent his Namesake HIRAM, or Huram, the most accomplish'd Mason upon Earth.

And the prodigious Expence of it also enhaunceth its Excellency; for besides King *David*'s vast Preparations, his richer Son SOLOMON, and all the wealthy *Israelites*, and the Nobles of all the neighbouring Kingdoms, largely contributed towards it in Gold, Silver, and rich Jewels, that amounted to a Sum almost incredible.

Nor do we read of any thing in *Canaan* so large, the Wall that inclos'd it being 7700 Foot in Compass; far less any holy Structure fit to be nam'd with it, for exactly proportion'd and beautiful Dimensions, from the magnificent *Porch* on the *East*, to the glorious and reverend *Sanctum Sanctorum* on the *West*, with most lovely and convenient Apartments for the *Kings* and *Princes*, *Priests* and *Levites*, *Israelites*, and *Gentiles* also; it being an House of Prayer for all Nations, and capable of receiving in the *Temple proper*, and in all its Courts and Apartments together, no less than 300,000 People, by a modest Calculation, allowing a square Cubit to each Person.

And if we consider the 1453 *Columns* of *Parian* Marble, with twice as many *Pillasters*, both having glorious *Capitals* of several Orders, and about 2246 *Windows*, besides those in the *Pavement*, with the unspeakable and costly *Decorations* of it within; *(and much more might be said)* we must conclude its Prospect to transcend our Imagination; and that it was justly esteem'd by far the finest Piece of *Masonry* upon Earth before or since, and the *chief Wonder* of the World; and was dedicated, or consecrated, in the most solemn manner, by *King* SOLOMON.

But leaving what must not, and indeed cannot, be communicated by Writing, we may warrantably affirm that however ambitious the *Heathen* were in cultivating of the *Royal Art*, it was never perfected, until God condescended to instruct his *peculiar People* in rearing the above-mention'd stately *Tent,* and in building at length this gorgeous *House,* fit for the special Refulgence of his *Glory,* where he dwelt between the *Cherubims* on the *Mercy-Seat,* and from thence gave them frequent oraculous Responses.

This most sumptuous, splendid, beautiful and glorious Edifice, attracted soon the inquisitive Artists of all Nations to spend some time at *Jerusalem,* and survey its peculiar Excellencies, as much as was allow'd to the *Gentiles;* whereby they soon discover'd, that all the World, with their joint Skill, came far short of the *Israelites,* in the Wisdom and Dexterity of *Architecture,* when the *wise King* SOLOMON was GRAND MASTER of the *Lodge* at *Jerusalem,* and the *learned King* HIRAM was GRAND MASTER of the *Lodge* at *Tyre,* and the *inspired* HIRAM ABIF was *Master of Work,* and *Masonry* was under the immediate Care and Direction of Heaven, when the *Noble* and the *Wise* thought it their Honour to be assisting to the ingenious *Masters* and *Craftsmen,* and when the *Temple* of the TRUE GOD became the Wonder of all Travellers, by which, as by the most perfect Pattern, they corrected the *Architecture* of their own Country upon their Return.

So that after the Erection of *Solomon's* Temple, *Masonry* was improv'd in all the neighbouring Nations; for the many Artists employed about it, under *Hiram Abif,* after it was finish'd, dispers'd themselves into *Syria, Mesopotamia, Assyria, Chaldea, Babylonia, Media, Persia, Arabia, Africa, Lesser Asia, Greece* and other Parts of *Europe,* where they taught this liberal Art to the *free born* Sons of eminent Persons, by whose Dexterity the Kings, Princes, and Potentates, built many glorious Piles, and became the GRAND MASTERS, each in his own Territory, and were emulous of excelling in this *Royal Art*; nay, even in INDIA, where the Correspondence was open, we may conclude the same: But none of the Nations, nor all together, could rival the *Israelites*, far less excel them, in *Masonry*; and their *Temple* remain'd the constant Pattern.

Franklin now traces a Masonic link through the ancient kings Nebuchadnezzar and Cyrus, to the Greek mathematicians Pythagoras and Euclid, to Ptolemy II, king of Egypt, to the Roman emperors Caesar and Augustus, to the temporary 'Dark Age' of Masonry during the decline of the Roman Empire. Masonry was preserved in England, Franklin claims, by the kings Athelstan and Alfred the Great; Henry VI carried on their good work and Masonry was kept alive by the Scottish kings. Elizabeth I, being a woman, was unqualified to become a Mason and actively 'discourag'd' the Craft, but when her successor James I (formerly James VI of Scotland) came to the throne, he brought the Scottish tradition of Masonry with him to England. Charles I was also a Mason, as was his son Charles II, under whom Christopher Wren, also a Mason, designed St

Paul's Cathedral. Strangely enough, Franklin does not claim James II, the infamous Catholic traitor to the (Protestant) Stuart dynasty, as a Mason, but assures us that once he was deposed, Masonry was restored to its rightful place of honour. Franklin brings the history up to date by assuring us that when George I, king of England when the original document on which Franklin is basing his *Constitutions* was written, laid the corner stone of the church of St Martin's in the Fields (near modern-day Trafalgar Square), he did so according to Masonic rites. Franklin ends thus:

In short, it would require many large Volumes to contain the many splendid Instances of the *mighty Influence* of Masonry from the Creation, in every Age, and in every Nation, as could be collected from Historians and Travellers: But especially in those Parts of the World where the Europeans correspond and trade, such Remains of ancient, large, curious, and magnificent *Colonading*, have been discover'd by the Inquisitive, that they can't enough lament the general Devastations of the *Goths* and *Mahometans*; and must conclude, that no *Art* was ever so much encourag'd as this; as indeed none other is so extensively useful to Mankind.

The next section of Franklin's text, *The Charges of a Free-Mason*, can be seen as something like a Masonic 'Ten Commandments':

The
# CHARGES
Of a FREE-MASON,
*Extracted from the ancient RECORDS of*
Lodges *beyond Sea, and of those in* England,
Scotland, *and* Ireland, *for the Use of the Lodges
in* London: *To be read at the making of* New
Brethren, *or when the Master shall order it.*
*The GENERAL HEADS, viz.*

I.   Of GOD and RELIGION.
II.  Of the CIVIL MAGISTRATE supreme and
     subordinate.
III. Of LODGES.
IV.  Of MASTERS, *Wardens, Fellows,* and *Apprentices.*
V.   Of the Management of the *Craft* in working.
VI.  Of BEHAVIOUR, *viz.*

    1. In the Lodge while *constituted.*
    2. After the Lodge is over and the *Brethren* not gone.
    3. When Brethren meet without *Strangers,* but not in
       a *Lodge.*
    4. In Presence of *Strangers not Masons.*
    5. At *Home,* and in the *Neighbourhood.*
    6. Towards a *strange Brother.*

## I. Concerning GOD and RELIGION.

A *Mason* is oblig'd by his Tenure, to obey the moral Law;
and if he rightly understands the Art, he will never be a

stupid *Atheist*, nor an irreligious *Libertine*. But though in ancient Times Masons were charg'd in every Country to be of the Religion of that Country or Nation, whatever it was, yet 'tis now thought more expedient only to oblige them to that Religion in which all Men agree, leaving their particular Opinions to themselves; that is, to be *good Men and true*, or Men of Honour and Honesty, by whatever Denominations or Persuasions they may be distinguish'd; whereby Masonry becomes the *Center* of *Union*, and the Means of conciliating true Friendship among Persons that must else have remain'd at a perpetual Distance.

## II. Of the CIVIL MAGISTRATE supreme and subordinate.

A *Mason* is a peaceable Subject to the Civil Powers, wherever he resides or works, and is never to be concern'd in Plots and Conspiracies against the Peace and Welfare of the Nation, nor to behave himself undutiful to inferior Magistrates; for as Masonry hath been always injured by War, Bloodshed, and Confusion, so ancient Kings and Princes have been much dispos'd to encourage the Craftsmen, because of their peaceableness and *Loyalty*, whereby they practically answer'd the Cavils of their Adversaries, and promoted the Honour of the Fraternity, who ever flourish'd in Times of Peace. So that if a Brother should be a Rebel against the State, he is not to be countenanc'd in his Rebellion, however he may be pitied as an unhappy Man; and if convicted of no other Crime, though the loyal

Brotherhood must and ought to disown his Rebellion, and give no Umbrage or Ground of political Jealousy to the Government for the time being; they cannot expel him from the *Lodge*, and his Relation to it remains indefeasible.

## III. Of LODGES.

A LODGE is a place where *Masons* assemble and work: Hence that Assembly, or duly organiz'd Society of Masons is call'd a LODGE, and every Brother ought to belong to one, and to be subject to its *By-Laws* and the GENERAL REGULATIONS. It is either *particular* or *general*, and will be best understood by attending it, and by the Regulations of the *General* or *Grand Lodge* hereunto annex'd. In ancient Times no *Master* or *Fellow* could be absent from it, especially when warn'd to appear at it, without incurring a severe Censure, until it appear to the *Master* and *Wardens*, that pure Necessity hinder'd him.

The Persons admitted Members of a *Lodge* must be good and true Men, free-born, and of mature and discreet Age, no Bondmen, no Women, no immoral or scandalous Men, but of good Report.

## IV. Of MASTERS, WARDENS, Fellows, and Apprentices.

All Preferment among *Masons* is grounded upon real Worth and personal Merit only; that so the *Lords* may be well served, the Brethren not put to Shame, nor the *Royal Craft* despis'd: Therefore no *Master* or *Warden* is chosen by Seniority, but for his Merit. It is impossible to describe these things in writing, and every Brother must attend in his Place, and learn them in a way peculiar to *this Fraternity*: Only *Candidates* may know, that no *Master* should take an *Apprentice*, unless he has sufficient Imployment for him, and unless he be a perfect Youth, having no Maim or Defect in his Body, that may render him uncapable of learning the *Art*, of serving his *Master's* LORD, and of being made a *Brother*, and then a *Fellow-Craft* in due time, even after he has served such a Term of Years as the Custom of the Country directs; and that he should be descended of honest Parents; that so, when otherwise qualify'd, he may arrive to the Honour of being the WARDEN, and then the *Master* of the *Lodge*, the *Grand Warden*, and at length the GRANDMASTER of all the *Lodges*, according to his Merit. [...]

## V. Of the Management of the CRAFT in working.

All *Masons* shall work honestly on working Days, that they may live creditably on *holy Days*; and the time appointed by the Law of the Land, or confirm'd by Custom, shall be observ'd.

The most expert of the *Fellow-Craftsmen* shall be chosen or appointed the *Master*, or Overseer of the *Lord's* Work; who is to be call'd MASTER by those that work under him. The *Craftsmen* are to avoid all ill Language, and to call each other by no disobliging Name, but *Brother* or *Fellow*; and to behave themselves courteously within and without the *Lodge*. The *Master*, knowing himself to be able of Cunning, shall undertake the *Lord*'s Work as reasonably as possible, and truly dispend his Goods as if they were his own; nor to give more Wages to any Brother or *Apprentice* than he really may deserve.

Both the *MASTER* and the *Masons* receiving their Wages justly, shall be faithful to the *Lord*, and honestly finish their Work, whether *Task* or *Journey*. Nor put the Work to *Task* that hath been accustomed to *Journey*. […]

# VI. Of BEHAVIOUR, viz.

### 1. In the LODGE while CONSTITUTED.

You are not to hold private Committees, or separate Conversation, without Leave from the *Master*, nor to talk of any thing impertinent or unseemly, nor interrupt the *Master* or *Wardens*, or any Brother speaking to the *Master*: Nor behave yourself ludicrously or jestingly while the *Lodge* is engaged in what is serious and solemn; nor use any unbecoming Language upon any Pretence whatsoever; but to pay due Reverence to your *Master*, *Wardens*, and *Fellows*, and put them to worship.

If any Complaint be brought, the Brother found guilty shall stand to the Award and Determination of the *Lodge*, who are the proper and competent Judges of all such Controversies, (unless you carry it by *Appeal* to the GRAND LODGE) and to whom they ought to be referr'd, unless a *Lord's* Work be hinder'd the mean while, in which Case a particular Reference may be made; but you must never go to Law about what concerneth *Masonry,* without an absolute Necessity apparent to the *Lodge.*

### 2. *BEHAVIOUR after the LODGE is over and the BRETHREN not gone.*

You may enjoy yourself with innocent Mirth, treating one another according to Ability, but avoiding all Excess, or forcing any Brother to eat or drink beyond his Inclination, or hindering him from going when his Occasions call him, or doing or saying anything offensive, or that may forbid an *easy* and *free* Conversation for that would blast our Harmony, and defeat our laudable Purposes. Therefore no private Piques or Quarrels must be brought within the Door of the *Lodge,* far less any Quarrels about *Religion,* or *Nations,* or *State-Policy,* we being only, as *Masons,* of the *Catholick Religion* above-mention'd; we are also of all *Nations, Tongues, Kindreds,* and *Languages,* and are resolv'd against all *Politicks,* as what never yet conduc'd to the Welfare of the *Lodge,* nor ever will. This *Charge* has been always strictly enjoin'd and observ'd; but especially ever since the *Reformation* in BRITAIN, or the Dissent and Secession of these Nations from the *Communion* of ROME.

### 3. BEHAVIOUR when Brethren meet without Strangers, but not in a LODGE form'd.

You are to salute one another in a courteous Manner, as you will be instructed, calling each other *Brother*, freely giving mutual Instruction as shall be thought expedient, without being overseen or overheard, and without encroaching upon each other, or derogating from that Respect which is due to any Brother, were he not a Mason: For though all *Masons* are as *Brethren* upon the same *Level*, yet *Masonry* takes no Honour from a Man that he had before; nay rather it adds to his Honour, especially if he has deserv'd well of the Brotherhood, who must give Honour to whom it is due, and avoid *ill Manners*.

### 4. BEHAVIOUR in the Presence of STRANGERS not MASONS.

You shall be cautious in your Words and Carriage, that the most penetrating Stranger shall not be able to discover or find out what is not proper to be intimated; and sometimes you shall divert a Discourse, and manage it prudently for the Honour of the *worshipful Fraternity*.

### 5. BEHAVIOUR at HOME, and in your NEIGHBOURHOOD.

You are to act as becomes a moral and wise Man; particularly, not to let your Family, Friends, and Neighbors know the *Concerns* of the *Lodge*, &c. but wisely to consult your own Honour, and that of the *ancient Brotherhood*, for

Reasons not to be mention'd here. You must also consult your Health, by not continuing together too late, or too long from home, after Lodge Hours are past; and by avoiding of Gluttony or Drunkenness, that your Families be not neglected or injured, nor you disabled from working.

### 6. *BEHAVIOUR towards a strange Brother.*
### *[i.e. a Mason whom you do not know]*

You are cautiously to examine him, in such a Method as Prudence shall direct you, that you may not be impos'd upon by an ignorant false *Pretender*, whom you are to reject with Contempt and Derision, and beware of giving him any Hints of Knowledge.

But if you discover him to be a true and genuine *Brother*, you are to respect him accordingly; and if he is in want, you must relieve him if you can, or else direct him how he may be reliev'd: You must employ him some Days, or else recommend him to be employ'd. But you are not charged to do beyond your Ability, only to prefer a poor *Brother*, that is a *good Man* and *true*, before any other poor People in the same Circumstances.

FINALLY, All these *CHARGES* you are to observe, and also those that shall be communicated to you in *another way*; cultivating BROTHERLY-LOVE, the Foundation and Cape-stone, the *Cement* and *Glory* of this ancient *Fraternity*, avoiding all Wrangling and Quarrelling, all Slander and Backbiting, nor permitting others to slander any honest Brother, but defending his Character, and doing him all good Offices, as far as is consistent with your *Honour* and *Safety*, and no farther. And if any of them do you Injury, you must apply to your own or his *Lodge* and from thence you may appeal to the GRAND LODGE at the *Quarterly Communication*, and from thence to the *annual* GRAND LODGE, as has been the ancient laudable Conduct of our Fore-fathers in every Nation; never taking a *legal Course* but when the Case cannot be otherwise decided, and patiently listening to the honest and friendly Advice of *Master* and *Fellows*, when they would prevent your going to Law with *Strangers*, or would excite you to put a speedy Period to all *Law-Suits*, that so you may mind the *Affair* of MASONRY with the more Alacrity and Success; but with respect to *Brothers* or *Fellows* at Law, the *Master* and Brethren should kindly offer their Mediation, which ought to be thankfully submitted to by the contending Brethren; and if that Submission is impracticable, they must however carry on their *Process* or *Law-Suit* without Wrath and Rancor (not in the common way) saying or doing nothing which may hinder *Brotherly Love*, and good Offices to be renew'd and continu'd; that all may see the *benign Influence* of MASONRY, as all true *Masons* have done from the Beginning of the *World*, and will do to the End of *Time*.

AMEN SO MOTE IT BE.

# DE QUINCEY'S THEORY

Thomas De Quincey, the well-known author of *Confessions of an Opium Eater* (1822), apparently didn't find Franklin's mythologised history of the Freemasons very plausible, and just two years after the publication of his most famous novel, he set about tracing the Freemasons to an earlier German society of mystics, the Rosicrucians. The Rosicrucians were concerned with, amongst other things, the secrets of alchemy and astronomy, and their debt to Freemasonry is marked in the title of the 18th degree of Scottish Rite Freemasonry: 'Knight of the Rose Croix'. The document that follows, De Quincey's *Historico-Critical Inquiry* (1824), begins by enumerating the many similarities between the Masons and the Rosicrucians.

# Historico-Critical Inquiry Into The Origin Of The Rosicrucians And The Free-Masons, Thomas de Quincey (1824)

*Chapter I. Of the essential characteristics of the orders of the Rosicrucians and the Free-Masons*

I deem it an indispensable condition of any investigation into the origin of the Rosicrucians and Free-masons that both orders should be surveyed comprehensively and in the whole compass of their relations and characteristic marks, not with reference to this or that mythos, symbol, usage, or form: and to the neglect of this condition, I believe, we must impute the unsuccessful issue which has hitherto attended the essays on this subject. First of all, therefore, I will assign those distinguishing features of these orders which appear to me universal and essential; and these I shall divide into *internal* and *external* – accordingly as they respect the personal relations and the purposes of their members, or simply the outward form of the institutions.

The universal and essential characteristics of the two orders, which come under the head of *internal*, are these which follow:-

I. As their fundamental maxim they assume – *Entire equality of personal rights amongst their members in relation to their final object.* All distinctions of social rank are annihilated. In the character of masons the

prince and the lowest citizen behave reciprocally
as free men – standing to each other in no relation
of civic inequality. This is a feature of masonry in
which it resembles the Church; projecting itself,
like *that* from the body of the State, and in idea
opposing itself to the State, though not in fact,
for, on the contrary, the ties of social obligation
are strengthened and sanctioned by the masonic
doctrines. It is true that these orders have degrees
– many or few according to the constitution of the
several mother-lodges. These, however, express no
subordination in rank or power: they imply simply a
more or less intimate connexion with the concerns
and purposes of the institution. A gradation of
this sort, corresponding to the different stages of
knowledge and initiation in the mysteries of the
order, was indispensable to the objects which they
had in view. It could not be advisable to admit
a young man, inexperienced and untried, to the
full participation of their secrets: he must first be
educated and moulded for the ends of the society.
Even elder men it was found necessary to subject to
the probation of the lower degrees before they were
admitted to the higher. Without such a regulation
dangerous persons might sometimes have crept
into the councils of the society; which, in fact,
happened occasionally in spite of all provisions
to the contrary. It may be alleged that this feature
of personal equality amongst the members in

relation to their private object is not exclusively the characteristic of Rosicrucians and Free-masons. True; it belongs no less to all the secret societies which have arisen in modern times. But, notwithstanding that, it is indisputable that to them was due the original scheme of an institution having neither an ecclesiastic nor a political tendency, and built on the personal equality of all the individuals who composed it.

II.  *Women, children, those who were not in the full possession of civic freedom, Jews, Anti-Christians generally, and* (according to undoubted historic documents), in the early days of these orders, *Roman Catholics were excluded from the society.* For what reason women were excluded, I suppose it can hardly be necessary to say. The absurd spirit of curiosity, talkativeness and levity, which distinguish that unhappy sex, were obviously incompatible with the grave purposes of the Rosicrucians and Masons. Not to mention that the familiar Intercourse, which co-membership in these societies brings along with it, would probably have led to some disorders in a promiscuous assemblage of both sexes, such as might have tainted the good fame or even threatened the existence of the order. More remarkable is the exclusion of *persons not wholly free*, of *Jews*, and of *anti-Christians*; and, indeed, it throws an important light upon the origin and character of the institutions. By *persons not free* we

are to understand not merely slaves and vassals,
but all those who were in the service of others
– and generally all who had not an independent
livelihood. Masonry presumes in all its members
the devotion of their knowledge and powers to
the objects of the institution. Now, what services
could be rendered by vassals, menial servants,
day-labourers, journeymen, with the limited means
at their disposal as to wealth or knowledge, and
in their state of dependency upon others? [...]
*Minors* were rejected unless when the consent of
their guardians was obtained; for otherwise the
order would have exposed itself to the suspicion
of tampering with young people in an illegal
way: to say nothing of the want of free-agency
in minors. [...] As to the exclusion of Anti-
Christians, especially of Jews, this may seem at
first sight inconsistent with the cosmo-political
tendency of Masonry. But had it that tendency at
its first establishment? Be this as it may, we need
not be surprised at such a regulation in an age so
little impressed with the virtue of toleration, and
indeed so little able – from political circumstances,
to practise it. Besides, it was necessary for their
own security; the Free-masons themselves were
exposed to a suspicion of atheism and sorcery;
and this suspicion would have been confirmed by
the indiscriminate admission of persons hostile to
Christianity. For the Jews in particular, there was

a further reason for rejecting them founded on the deep degradation of the national character. With respect to the Roman Catholics, I need not at this point anticipate the historic data which favour their exclusion. The fact is certain; but, I add, only for the earlier periods of Free-masonry. Further on, the cosmo-political constitution of the order had cleared it of all such religious tests; and at this day, I believe, that in the lodges of London and Paris there would be no hesitation in receiving as a brother any upright Mohammedan or Jew. Even in smaller cities, where lingering prejudices would still cleave with more bigotry to the old exclusions, greater stress is laid upon the natural religion of the candidate – his belief in God and his sense of moral obligation – than upon his positive confession of faith. In saying this, however, I would not be understood to speak of certain individual sects among the Rosicrucians, whose mysticism leads them to demand special religious qualities in their proselytes which are dispensed with by common Free-masonry.

III. *The orders make pretensions to mysteries.* These relate partly to ends and partly to means, and are derived from the East, whence they profess to derive an occult wisdom not revealed to the profane. This striving after hidden knowledge, it was, that specially distinguished these societies from others that pursued unknown objects. And, because their main object was a mystery, and that it might remain such, an oath of secrecy was demanded of every member on his admission. Nothing of this mystery could ever be discovered by a visit from the police; for, when such an event happens, and naturally it has happened many times, the business is at an end – and the lodge *ipso facto* dissolved; besides that all the acts of the members are symbolic, and unintelligible to all but the initiated. Meantime no government can complain of this exclusion from the mysteries: as every governor has it at his own option to make himself fully acquainted with them by procuring his own adoption into the society. This it is which in most countries has gradually reconciled the supreme authorities to Masonic Societies, hard as the persecution was which they experienced at first. Princes and prelates made themselves brothers of the order as the condition of admission to the mysteries. And, think what they would of these mysteries in other respects, they found nothing in them which could justify any hostility on the part of the State.

In an examination of Masonic and Rosicrucian Societies the weightiest question is that which regards the nature of those mysteries. To this question we must seek for a key in the spirit of that age when the societies themselves originated. We shall thus learn, first of all, whether these societies do in reality cherish any mystery as the final object of their researches; and, secondly, perhaps we shall thus come to understand the extraordinary fact that the Rosicrucian and Masonic secret should not long ago have been betrayed in spite of the treachery which we must suppose in a certain proportion of those who were parties to that secret in every age.

IV. *These orders have a general system of signs* (e.g. that of recognition), *usages, symbols, mythi, and festivals.* In this place it may be sufficient to say generally that even that part of the ritual and mythology which is already known to the public will be found to confirm the conclusions drawn from other historical data as to the origin and purpose of the institution. Thus, for instance, we may be assured beforehand that the original Free-masons must have had some reason for appropriating to themselves the attributes and emblems of real handicraft Masons: which part of their ritual they are so far from concealing that in London they often parade on solemn occasions attired in full costume. As little can it be imagined that the selection of the feast of St. John (Midsummer-day) as their own chief festival was at first arbitrary and without a significant import.

Of the *external* characteristics or those which the society itself announces to the world the main is the *public profession of beneficence*; not to the brothers only, though of course to them more especially, but also to strangers. And it cannot be denied by those who are least favourably disposed to the order of Free-masons that many states in Europe, where lodges have formerly existed or do still exist, are indebted to them for the original establishment of many salutary institutions having for their object the mitigation of human suffering. The other external characteristics are properly negative, and are these:

I.  *Masonry is compatible with every form of civil constitution;* which cosmo-political relation of the order to every mode and form of social arrangements has secured the possibility of its reception amongst all nations, however widely separated in policy and laws.

II.  *It does not impose celibacy:* and this is the criterion that distinguishes it from the religious orders, and from many of the old knightly orders, in which celibacy was an indispensable law, or still is so.

III.  *It enjoins no peculiar dress* (except indeed in the official assemblages of the lodges, for the purpose of marking the different degrees), *no marks of distinction in the ordinary commerce of life, and no abstinence from civil offices and business.* Here again is a remarkable distinction from the religious and knightly orders.

IV.  It *grants to every member a full liberty to dissolve his connection with the order at any time, and without even acquainting the superiors of the lodge:* though of course he cannot release himself from the obligation of his vow of secrecy. Nay, even after many years of voluntary separation from the order, a return to it is always allowed. In the religious and knightly orders the members have not the powers, excepting under certain circumstances, of leaving them; and, under no circumstances, of returning. This last was a politic regulation; for, whilst on one hand the society was sufficiently secured by the oath of secrecy, on the other hand, by the easiness of the yoke which it imposed, it could the more readily attract members. A young man might enter the order, satisfy himself as to the advantages that were to be expected from it, and leave it upon further experience or any revolution in his own way of thinking. [...]

Rosicrucianism, it is true, is not Free-masonry: but the latter borrowed its form from the first. He that gives himself out for a Rosicrucian, without knowing the general ritual of masonry, is unquestionably an impostor. Some peculiar sects there are which adopt certain follies and chimeras of the Rosicrucians (as gold-making); and to these he may belong; but a legitimate Rosicrucian, in the original sense and spirit of the order, he cannot be.

## A MASONIC HOAX

Léo Taxil (1854–1907), a French writer and journalist, was also the originator of one of the best-known rumours that surround Freemasonry: that Masons are closet Satanists. Taxil's first work, *La bible Amusante*, was an anti-Catholic satire, and his later work, *Les Pornographes sacrés: la confession et les confesseurs*, claimed that senior French clergy indulged in hedonistic, fetishistic orgies. Later in his life, Taxil turned his satirical attentions to Freemasonry, and wrote several pamphlets that

*Léo Taxil*

*Poster advertising the books of Taxil. The winged goat-man figure*
*wearing the apron of the Knights Templar is Baphomet*

suggested that the Freemasons worshipped a god called 'Baphomet', who was both male and female, both animal and human. To back up his theory, he drew upon a quotation by the eminent populariser of American Scottish Rite Freemasonry, Albert Pike (1809–91), who is recorded as saying 'Lucifer is God'. (We will return to Pike in Chapter V.) The Masons were also implicated with Satanism due to the publication of one of the rituals of the York Rite (see Chapter VI), that of the 'Holy Royal Arch'. As part of this ritual, a Holy Word is revealed that is described as another name for God: Jahbulon (pronounced 'Yahbulon'). The word is explained as originating from three names for God in three ancient religious traditions: Jah from the Hebrew Yahweh, Bul from the Syriac Baal, and On from the Egyptian Osiris. The name of Baal occurs many times in the Old Testament to describe the pagan god of the Phoenicians and has become akin to Satan or the Devil. Despite these two minor connections with Satanism, Freemasonry cannot truly be said to be obviously affiliated with the Occult, and Taxil eventually revealed his findings to be a hoax, but not before the myth that he created had passed into legend.

*An illustration plate of an alleged Masonic ritual from Taxil's*
The Devil In The Nineteenth Century

# THE STONEMASONS OF SOLOMON'S TEMPLE

One of the pivotal Masonic myths that has already been touched on in the initiation ceremonies from *Duncan's Ritual and Monitor of Freemasonry*, as well as in Franklin's *Constitutions*, is the symbolism of Solomon's Temple. Solomon is thought of as the first Masonic Worshipful Master, and the layout of every Masonic lodge echoes his Temple. Some, notably Adolf Hitler, who sent an estimated 80,000 to 200,000 Freemasons to their deaths in concentration camps, have seen the Masons as a proto-Zionist organisation, but the Masonic use of the symbolism of the Temple of Solomon is not proselytising; it is merely part of Masonic mythological tradition. The following text by Albert G. Mackey, published in New York in 1882, explains the symbolic significance that the Mason-led construction of the Temple, as well as its finished form, has for Freemasons:

# THE
# SYMBOLISM OF FREEMASONRY:
### ILLUSTRATING AND EXPLAINING
### Its Science and Philosophy, its Legends, Myths, and Symbols.

BY

## ALBERT G. MACKEY, M. D.,

AUTHOR OF "LEXICON OF FREEMASONRY," "TEXT-BOOK OF
MASONIC JURISPRUDENCE;" "CRYPTIC MASONRY;"
ETC.; ETC.

## The symbolism of Solomon's Temple

I HAVE said that the operative art is symbolized – that is to say, used as a symbol – in the speculative science. Let us now inquire, as the subject of the present essay, how this is done in reference to a system of symbolism dependent for its construction on types and figures derived from the temple of Solomon, and which we hence call the "Temple Symbolism of Freemasonry." [...]

Now, the operative art having, *for us*, ceased, we, as speculative Masons, symbolize the labors of our predecessors by engaging in the construction of a spiritual temple in our hearts, pure and spotless, fit for the dwelling-place of Him who is the author of purity – where God is to be worshipped in spirit and in truth, and whence every evil thought and unruly passion is to be banished, as the sinner and the Gentile were excluded from the sanctuary of the Jewish temple.

This spiritualizing of the temple of Solomon is the first, the most prominent and most pervading of all the symbolic instructions of Freemasonry. It is the link that binds the operative and speculative divisions of the order. It is this which gives it its religious character. Take from Freemasonry its dependence on the temple, leave out of its ritual all reference to that sacred edifice, and to the legends connected with it, and the system itself must at once decay and die, or at best remain only as some fossilized bone, imperfectly to show the nature of the living body to which it once belonged.

Temple worship is in itself an ancient type of the religious sentiment in its progress towards spiritual elevation. As soon as a nation emerged, in the world's progress, out of Fetichism, or the worship of visible objects, – the most degraded form of idolatry, – its people began to establish a priesthood and to erect temples. [...]

I propose now to illustrate, by a few examples, the method in which the speculative Masons have appropriated this design of King Solomon to their own use. To construct his earthly temple, the operative mason followed the architectural designs laid down on the *trestle-board*, or tracing-board, or book of plans of the architect. By these he hewed and squared his materials; by these he raised his walls; by these he constructed his arches; and by these strength and durability, combined with grace and beauty, were bestowed upon the edifice which he was constructing.

The trestle-board becomes, therefore, one of our

elementary symbols. For in the masonic ritual the speculative Mason is reminded that, as the operative artist erects his temporal building, in accordance with the rules and designs laid down on the trestle-board of the master workman, so should he erect that spiritual building, of which the material is a type, in obedience to the rules and designs, the precepts and commands, laid down by the grand Architect of the universe, in those great books of nature and revelation, which constitute the spiritual trestle-board of every Freemason.

The trestle-board is, then, the symbol of the natural and moral law. Like every other symbol of the order, it is universal and tolerant in its application; and while, as Christian Masons, we cling with unfaltering integrity to that explanation which makes the Scriptures of both dispensations our trestle-board, we permit our Jewish and Mohammedan brethren to content themselves with the books of the Old Testament, or the Koran. Masonry does not interfere with the peculiar form or development of any one's religious faith. All that it asks is that the interpretation of the symbol shall be according to what each one supposes to be the revealed will of his Creator. But so rigidly exacting is it that the symbol shall be preserved, and, in some rational way, interpreted, that it peremptorily excludes the Atheist from its communion, because, believing in no Supreme Being, no divine Architect, he must necessarily be without a spiritual trestle-board on which the designs of that Being may be inscribed for his direction.

But the operative mason required materials wherewith to construct his temple. There was, for instance, the *rough ashlar* – the stone in its rude and natural state – unformed and unpolished, as it had been lying in the quarries of Tyre from the foundation of the earth. This stone was to be hewed and squared, to be fitted and adjusted, by simple, but appropriate implements, until it became a *perfect ashlar*, or well-finished stone, ready to take its destined place in the building.

Here, then, again, in these materials do we find other elementary symbols. The rough and unpolished stone is a symbol of man's natural state – ignorant, uncultivated, and, as the Roman historian expresses it, "grovelling to the earth, like the beasts of the field, and obedient to every sordid appetite;" – but when education has exerted its salutary influences in expanding his intellect, in restraining his hitherto unruly passions, and purifying his life, he is then represented by the perfect ashlar, or finished stone, which, under the skilfull hands of the workman, has been smoothed, and squared, and fitted for its appropriate place in the building.

Here an interesting circumstance in the history of the preparation of these materials has been seized and beautifully appropriated by our symbolic science. We learn from the account of the temple, contained in the First Book of Kings, that "The house, when it was in building, was built of stone, made ready before it was brought thither, so that there was neither hammer nor axe, nor any tool of iron, heard in the house while it was in building."

Now, this mode of construction, undoubtedly adopted to avoid confusion and discord among so many thousand workmen, has been selected as an elementary symbol of concord and harmony — virtues which are not more essential to the preservation and perpetuity of our own society than they are to that of every human association.

The perfect ashlar, therefore, — the stone thus fitted for its appropriate position in the temple, — becomes not only a symbol of human perfection (in itself, of course, only a comparative term), but also, when we refer to the mode in which it was prepared, of that species of perfection which results from the concord and union of men in society. It is, in fact, a symbol of the social character of the institution.

There are other elementary symbols, to which I may hereafter have occasion to revert; the three, however, already described, — the rough ashlar, the perfect ashlar, and the trestle-board, — and which, from their importance, have received the name of "jewels," will be sufficient to give some idea of the nature of what may be called the "symbolic alphabet" of Masonry. Let us now proceed to a brief consideration of the method in which this alphabet of the science is applied to the more elevated and abstruser portions of the system, and which, as the temple constitutes its most important type, I have chosen to call the "Temple Symbolism of Masonry."

Both Scripture and tradition inform us that, at the building of King Solomon's temple, the masons were divided into different classes, each engaged in different tasks. We learn, from the Second Book of Chronicles, that these classes were the bearers of burdens, the hewers of stones, and the overseers, called by the old masonic writers the *Ish sabal*, the *Ish chotzeb*, and the *Menatzchim*. Now, without pretending to say that the modern institution has preserved precisely the same system of regulations as that which was observed at the temple, we shall certainly find a similarity in these divisions to the Apprentices, Fellow Crafts and Master Masons of our own day. At all events, the three divisions made by King Solomon in the workmen at Jerusalem have been adopted as the types of the three degrees now practised in speculative Masonry; and as such we are, therefore, to consider them. The mode in which these three divisions of workmen labored in constructing the temple has been beautifully symbolized in speculative Masonry, and constitutes an important and interesting part of temple symbolism.

Thus we know, from our own experience among modern workmen, who still pursue the same method, as well as from the traditions of the order, that the implements used in the quarries were few and simple, the work there requiring necessarily, indeed, but two tools, namely, the *twenty-four inch gauge*, or two foot rule, and the *common gavel*, or stone-cutter's hammer. With the former implement, the operative mason took the necessary dimensions of the stone he was about to prepare, and with the latter, by repeated blows, skilfully applied, he broke off every unnecessary protuberance, and rendered it smooth and square, and fit to take its place in the building.

And thus, in the first degree of speculative Masonry, the Entered Apprentice receives these simple implements, as the emblematic working tools of his profession, with their appropriate symbolical instruction. To the operative mason their mechanical and practical use alone is signified, and nothing more of value does their presence convey to his mind. To the speculative Mason the sight of them is suggestive of far nobler and sublimer thoughts; they teach him to measure, not stones, but time; not to smooth and polish the marble for the builder's use, but to purify and cleanse his heart from every vice and imperfection that would render it unfit for a place in the spiritual temple of his body. [...]

At the building, of the temple, the stones having been thus prepared by the workmen of the lowest degree (the Apprentices, as we now call them, the aspirants of the ancient Mysteries), we are informed that they were transported to the site of the edifice on Mount Moriah, and were there placed in the hands of another class of workmen, who are now technically called the Fellow Crafts, and who correspond to the Mystes, or those who had received the second degree of the ancient Mysteries. At this stage of the operative work more extensive and important labors were to be performed, and accordingly a greater amount of skill and knowledge was required of those to whom these labors were intrusted. The stones, having been prepared by the Apprentices (for hereafter, in speaking of the workmen of the temple, I shall use the equivalent appellations of the more modern Masons), were now to be deposited in their destined places in the building, and the massive walls were to be erected. For these purposes implements of a higher and more complicated character than the gauge and gavel were necessary. The *square* was required to fit the joints with sufficient accuracy, the *level* to run the courses in a horizontal line, and the *plumb* to erect the whole with due regard to perfect perpendicularity. This portion of the labor finds its symbolism in the second degree of the speculative science, and in applying this symbolism we still continue to refer to the idea of erecting a spiritual temple in the heart.

The necessary preparations, then, having been made in the first degree, the lessons having been received by which the aspirant is taught to commence the labor of life with the purification of the heart, as a Fellow Craft he continues the task by cultivating those virtues which give form and impression to the character, as well adapted stones give shape and stability to the building. And hence the "working tools" of the Fellow Craft are referred, in their symbolic application, to those virtues. In the alphabet of symbolism, we find the square, the level, and the plumb appropriated to this second degree. The square is a symbol denoting morality. It teaches us to apply the unerring principles of moral science to every action of our lives, to see that all the motives and results of our conduct shall coincide with the dictates of divine justice, and that all our thoughts, words, and deeds shall harmoniously conspire, like the well-adjusted and rightly squared joints of an edifice, to produce a smooth, unbroken life of virtue.

The plumb is a symbol of rectitude of conduct, and inculcates that integrity of life and undeviating course of moral uprightness which can alone distinguish the good and just man. As the operative workman erects his temporal building with strict observance of that plumb-line, which will not permit him to deviate a hair's breadth to the right or to the left, so the speculative Mason, guided by the unerring principles of right and truth inculcated in the symbolic teachings of the same implement, is steadfast in the pursuit of truth, neither bending beneath the frowns of adversity nor yielding to the seductions of prosperity.

The level, the last of the three working tools of the operative craftsman, is a symbol of equality of station. Not that equality of civil or social position which is to be found only in the vain dreams of the anarchist or the Utopian, but that great moral and physical equality which affects the whole human race as the children of one common Father, who causes his sun to shine and his rain to fall on all alike, and who has so appointed the universal lot of humanity, that death, the leveller of all human greatness, is made to visit with equal pace the prince's palace and the peasant's hut.

[...] We now reach the third degree, the Master Masons of the modern science, and the Epopts, or beholders of the sacred things in the ancient Mysteries.

In the third degree the symbolic allusions to the temple

of Solomon, and the implements of Masonry employed in its construction, are extended and fully completed. At the building of that edifice, we have already seen that one class of the workmen was employed in the preparation of the materials, while another was engaged in placing those materials in their proper position. But there was a third and higher class, – the master workmen, – whose duty it was to superintend the two other classes, and to see that the stones were not only duly prepared, but that the most exact accuracy had been observed in giving to them their true juxtaposition in the edifice. It was then only that the last and finishing labor was performed, and the cement was applied by these skilful workmen, to secure the materials in their appropriate places, and to unite the building in one enduring and connected mass. Hence the *trowel*, we are informed, was the most important, though of course not the only, implement in use among the master builders. They did not permit this last, indelible operation to be performed by any hands less skilful than their own. They required that the craftsmen should prove the correctness of their work by the square, level, and plumb, and test, by these unerring instruments, the accuracy of their joints; and, when satisfied of the just arrangement of every part, the cement, which was to give an unchangeable union to the whole, was then applied by themselves.

Hence, in speculative Masonry, the trowel has been assigned to the third degree as its proper implement, and the symbolic meaning which accompanies it has a strict and beautiful reference to the purposes for which it was used in the ancient temple; for as it was there employed "to spread the cement which united the building in one common mass," so is it selected as the symbol of brotherly love – that cement whose object is to unite our mystic association in one sacred and harmonious band of brethren.

Here, then, we perceive the first, or, as I have already called it, the elementary form of our symbolism – the adaptation of the terms, and implements, and processes of an operative art to a speculative science. The temple is now completed. The stones having been hewed, squared, and numbered in the quarries by the apprentices, – having been properly adjusted by the craftsmen, and finally secured in their appropriate places, with the strongest and purest cement, by the master builders, – the temple of King Solomon presented, in its finished condition, so noble an appearance of sublimity and grandeur as to well deserve to be selected, as it has been, for the type or symbol of that immortal temple of the body, to which Christ significantly and symbolically alluded when he said, "Destroy this temple, and in three days I will raise it up."

[...]

The idea, therefore, of making the temple a symbol of the body, is not exclusively masonic; but the mode of treating the symbolism by a reference to the particular temple of Solomon, and to the operative art engaged in its construction, is peculiar to Freemasonry. It is this which isolates it from all other similar associations. Having many things in common with the secret societies and religious Mysteries of antiquity, in this "temple symbolism" it differs from them all.

## The form of the Lodge

IN the last essay, I treated of that symbolism of the masonic system which makes the temple of Jerusalem the archetype of a lodge, and in which, in consequence, all the symbols are referred to the connection of a speculative science with an operative art. I propose in the present to discourse of a higher and abstruser mode of symbolism; and it may be observed that, in coming to this topic, we arrive, for the first time, at that chain of resemblances which unites Freemasonry with the ancient systems of religion, and which has given rise, among masonic writers, to the names of Pure and Spurious Freemasonry – the pure Freemasonry being that system of philosophical religion which, coming through the line of the patriarchs, was eventually modified by influences exerted at the building of King Solomon's temple, and the spurious being the same system as it was altered and corrupted by the polytheism of the nations of heathendom.

As this abstruser mode of symbolism, if less peculiar to the masonic system, is, however, far more interesting than the one which was treated in the previous essay, – because it is more philosophical, – I propose to give an extended investigation of its character. And, in the first place, there is what may be called an elementary view of this abstruser symbolism, which seems almost to be a corollary from what has already been described in the preceding article.

As each individual mason has been supposed to be the symbol of a spiritual temple, – "a temple not made with hands, eternal in the heavens," – the lodge or collected assemblage of these masons is adopted as a symbol of the world.

[...] The form of a masonic lodge is said to be a parallelogram, or oblong square; its greatest length being from east to west, its breadth from north to south. A square, a circle, a triangle, or any other form but that of an *oblong square* would be eminently incorrect and unmasonic, because such a figure would not be an expression of the symbolic idea which is intended to be conveyed.

Now, as the world is a globe, or, to speak more accurately, an oblate spheroid, the attempt to make an oblong square its symbol would seem, at first view, to present insuperable difficulties. But the system of masonic symbolism has stood the test of too long an experience to be easily found at fault; and therefore this very symbol furnishes a striking evidence of the antiquity of the order. At the Solomonic era – the era of the building of the temple at Jerusalem – the world, it must be remembered, was supposed to have that very oblong form, which has been here symbolized. If, for instance, on a map of the world we should inscribe an oblong figure whose boundary lines would circumscribe and include just that portion which was known to be inhabited in the days of Solomon, these lines, running a short distance north and south of the Mediterranean Sea, and extending from Spain in the west to Asia Minor in the east, would form an oblong square, including the southern shore of Europe, the northern shore of Africa, and the western district of Asia, the length of the parallelogram being about sixty degrees from east to west, and its breadth being about twenty degrees from north to south. This oblong square, thus enclosing the whole of what was then supposed to be the habitable globe, would precisely represent what is symbolically said to be *the form of the lodge*, while the Pillars of Hercules in the west, on each side of the straits of Gades or Gibraltar, might appropriately be referred to the two pillars that stood at the porch of the temple.

A masonic lodge is, therefore, a symbol of the world. This symbol is sometimes, by a very usual figure of speech, extended, in its application, and the world and the universe are made synonymous, when the lodge becomes, of course, a symbol of the universe. But in this case the definition of the symbol is extended, and to the ideas of length and breadth are added those of height and depth, and the lodge is said to assume the form of a double cube. The solid contents of the earth below and the expanse of the heavens above will then give the outlines of the cube, and the whole created universe will be included within the symbolic limits of a mason's lodge.

By always remembering that the lodge is the symbol, in its form and extent, of the world, we are enabled, readily and rationally, to explain many other symbols attached principally to the first degree; and we are enabled to collate and compare them with similar symbols of other kindred institutions of antiquity, for it should be observed that this symbolism of the world, represented by a place of initiation, widely pervaded all the ancient rites and mysteries.

## ◆ CHAPTER III ◆

# George Washington, Master Mason

**B**enjamin Franklin's devotion to the Masonic cause has already been seen, but America's Masonic fraternity boasts an even more illustrious member: George Washington. Washington was initiated at the Fredericksburg Lodge of Ancient, Free and Accepted Masons No. 4, Virginia, as an Entered Apprentice on 4 November 1752, and climbed the ranks to Master Mason in less than nine months. He remained a Mason throughout his life and was even buried according to Masonic ritual. Washington donned his apron on many ceremonial occasions, including when laying the corner-stone of the Capitol Building in accordance with Masonic rites on 18 September 1793. There are two famous aprons that were worn by Washington, the first of which is known as the Watson Cassoul Apron, presented to Washington in January 1782 by Elkanah Watson of Plymouth, Massachusetts, and Monsieur Cassoul, originally from Nantes, France. It is, however, the second apron that is the more famous: a gift from the key figure in the French and American revolutions, Gilbert Lafayette. It was this apron that Washington wore when laying the corner-stone of the Capitol Building. Embroidered on white satin by Lafayette's wife, the apron was presented to Washington in August 1784. An engraving of the apron, which was originally lined with bright blue and red ribbon and embroidered in coloured silk thread throughout, appears opposite.

## WASHINGTON'S MASONIC APRON

The significance of the emblems on this apron can reveal much about the symbolism of Freemasonry.

The use of red, white and blue trim has no Masonic significance, but echoes the shared national colours of France and the newly established United States.

The apron's 'mark' motif, placed on the downward fold of the Master Mason's apron, is that of a beehive, which symbolises industry – from *Duncan's Ritual and Monitor*: '[The beehive] teaches us that, as we come into the world rational and intelligent beings, so we should ever be industrious ones; never sitting down contented

while our fellow-creatures around us are in want, when it is in our power to relieve them without inconvenience to ourselves.' The letters that surround the beehive are used in the Mark Master's degree in the York Rite (see Chapter V).

The All-Seeing Eye at the top of the main section of the apron represents The Great Architect of the Universe, who 'beholds the inmost recesses of the human heart, and will reward us according to our works'.

In the centre of the main section lie, appropriately enough, the central symbols of Freemasonry: the Square and Compasses, lying on the Volume of Sacred Law (which is the Bible in most Masonic lodges). The Square, Compasses and Volume of Sacred Law are known as the three Great Lights of Freemasonry. The Square is a working tool of a Fellow-Craft Mason, and described in *The Symbolism of Freemasonry* as 'a symbol denoting morality. It teaches us to apply the unerring principles of moral science to every action of our lives, to see that all the motives and results of our conduct shall coincide with the dictates of divine justice, and that all our thoughts, words, and deeds shall harmoniously conspire, like the well-adjusted and rightly squared joints of an edifice, to produce a smooth, unbroken life of virtue'. The compasses are a working tool of a Master Mason, with which Masons learn to 'circumscribe their desires and keep their passions within due bounds toward all mankind'. Other Masonic tools and symbols such as the trowel, ladder and maul surround the Square and Compasses in the central portion of the apron.

The six steps up to the Great Lights of Freemasonry traditionally number three in Masonic symbolism, and some have speculated that Lafayette included six steps to indicate that Washington had not just reached the third rank, of Master Mason, but had also advanced to the sixth degree in the York Rite, that of *Most Excellent Master*.

The two larger, outer pillars represent the pillars of Enoch, one made out of marble in order to resist fire and one of brass in order to resist water. The inner pillars represent Boaz and Jachin, the two pillars that flanked Solomon's temple, whose symbolism is critical to the Fellow Craft initiation ceremony detailed in Chapter I.

Finally, the coffin at the bottom of the apron is a symbol for death and reminiscent of the symbolic death of a Mason playing the part of the murdered Hiram Abiff in the initiation into the third degree of Master Mason. The sprig of acacia that arises from the coffin is traditionally strewn over the coffins of Masons who have departed for the celestial lodge above.

## WASHINGTON: A MASONIC LIFE

Washington's association with Freemasonry is usually a subject his biographers gloss over, and one of the earliest attempts to rectify this imbalance was a book published in 1866 entitled *Washington and his Masonic compeers*, which not only gives a full account of Washington's dealings with Masonry, but also elucidates the importance of Masonry to a number of other key figures of early American history, including Benjamin Franklin, John Sullivan, Major-General of the Revolution, and Dr Samuel Seabury, the first Episcopal bishop in America.

# WASHINGTON
# AND HIS
# MASONIC COMPEERS
## BY
## SIDNEY HAYDEN
### PAST MASTER OF RURAL AMITY LODGE, No. 70,
### PENNSYLVANIA

*Preface*

------------

BIOGRAPHIES of WASHINGTON, and the most eminent of our countrymen who were contemporary with him, have been often written so far as relates to their public acts, and in many of them we have also a portraiture of their personal and domestic history.

Our historians and biographers seldom mention a Fraternity which has existed in this country from its early colonial existence, and embraced in its membership a large number of our countrymen whose names are inscribed on our literary, civil, and military rolls of honor. Has this arisen from a prejudice against the institution of Masonry, or from a belief that its influences are unimportant? […]

WASHINGTON, with a full knowledge of the subject, wrote: "Being persuaded that a just application of the principles on which the Masonic Fraternity is founded must be promotive of virtue and public prosperity, I shall always be happy to advance the interest of the Society, and be considered by them a deserving brother."

## Chapter I

[Washington is initiated into Masonry]

[...] WASHINGTON then was nineteen years of age, and held the position of adjutant-general in the Virginia militia, with the rank of major. He was said by his contemporaries at this period of his life to be grave, silent, and thoughtful, diligent and methodical in business, dignified in his appearance, strictly honorable in all his actions, and a stranger to dissipation and riot. Such was his early history and character when, in 1752, in the twenty-first year of his age, he offered himself to Fredericksburg Lodge as a candidate for the mysteries of Masonry.

## Chapter II

[Washington rises through the Masonic ranks]

[...] Before WASHINGTON came to manhood, a lodge had been organized in Fredericksburg, under authority from THOMAS OXNARD, Provincial Grand Master at Boston, whose authority also extended over all the English colonies in America. [...] The records of Fredericksburg Lodge show the presence of WASHINGTON, for the first time in the lodge, on the fourth of November, 5752, leaving no doubt that he was initiated on that day, as on the 6th of November, the record continues, "Received of Mr. GEORGE WASHINGTON for his entrance £2:3."

"March 3d, 5753 GEORGE WASHINGTON passed Fellow Craft."

"August 4th, 5753 GEORGE WASHINGTON raised Master Mason."

The old record-book of the lodge is still preserved; also the Bible on which he was obligated, and the seal of the lodge. The Bible is a small quarto volume, and bears date, "Cambridge, printed by John Field, printer to the University, 1688." The seal is beautifully engraved, having for its principal device a shield crested with a castle, with castles also on each of its points, with compasses in its centre. Below the shield is the motto, "IN THE LORD is ALL OUR TRUST" the whole surrounded with "FREDERICKSBURGH LODGE," in a circle.

Had the lodge at Fredericksburg known how deep an interest would be felt by succeeding generations in all that pertained to WASHINGTON, his Masonic record, even at that period, would probably have been made with more fulness of detail; and yet its very conciseness is confirmatory proof, if such were needed, of the verity of the facts there recorded. The lessons of history are progressive, and none could have known, as he passed through the mystic rites of Masonry in 1752, in presence of that chosen band of brethren in Fredericksburg Lodge, that the new-made brother then before them would win, in after-years, a nation's honor, gratitude, and love; and that when a century had passed, the anniversary of his initiation would be celebrated as a national Masonic jubilee.

## Chapter III

### [Washington put forward as Grand Master of Virginia Lodge and becomes a household name of American Masonry]

The commencement of the American Revolution was a new era in the Masonic as well as political history of our country. As the biographer of WASHINGTON'S public history is obliged to trace it along the pathway of current public events, so also his Masonic life, when fully given, must be blended with the Masonic history of the times in which he lived. From the first introduction of warranted lodges into America in 1733, until the commencement of the Revolution, Masonry had been in a state of progress in this country, so that in 1774 there were three warranted lodges in each of the thirteen colonies, and in seven of them Provincial Grand Lodges.

[...]

For the leading idea of the symbolism of the chain representing the union of the colonies, the brethren were probably indebted to Dr. FRANKLIN, who visited the American camp in 1776 [...] and the seal is supposed to have been engraved by PAUL REVERE, a distinguished Mason and patriot of Massachusetts.

[...]

Virginia called a convention of its lodges, which recommended to its constituents GEORGE WASHINGTON as the most proper person to be elected the first independent Grand Master of Virginia. WASHINGTON at that time had held no official position in Masonry, and he modestly declined the intended honor, when informed of the wish of his Virginia brethren, for two reasons: first, he did not consider it masonically legal, that one who had never been installed as Master or Warden of a lodge should be elected Grand Master; and second, his country claimed at the time all his services in the tended field. JOHN BLAIR, therefore, the Master of Williamsburg Lodge, who was an eminent citizen of Virginia, was elected in his stead.

[...]

WASHINGTON visited Philadelphia, where Congress was in session; and while there, the Grand Lodge of Pennsylvania celebrated the festival of St. John the Evangelist. WASHINGTON was present on the occasion, and was honoured with the chief place in the procession, being supported on his right by the Grand Master, and on his left by the Deputy Grand Master. More than three hundred brethren joined in the procession.

[...]

We have no doubt, from this time onward it was the desire of many of the brethren, especially those in the army, to see WASHINGTON placed at the head of American Masonry. At a public festival of American Union Lodge, held at Reading, in Connecticut, on the 25th of March, 1779, the first toast given was "GENERAL WASHINGTON;" which was followed by one to *The memory of* WARREN, MONTGOMERY, *and* WOOSTER," three distinguished Masons who had fallen on the battle-fields of the Revolution. From this time onward the name of WASHINGTON became a Masonic toast, and the first in order at all Masonic festivals.

### Chapter IV

[Washington is put forward to be the Grand Master of the entire United States]

At the close of 1779, WASHINGTON'S headquarters were again at Morristown, New Jersey, where they had been during the winter of 1776–77. Here the American Union Lodge was again at work, and also various other military lodges, which had been organized in the American army. On the 27th of December, the American Union Lodge met to celebrate the festival of St. John the Evangelist. Besides the regular members of the lodge present, the record shows the names of sixty-eight visiting brethren, one of whom was WASHINGTON. [...] At the festival meeting on the 27th, "a petition was read, representing the present state of Free-Masonry to the several Deputy Grand Masters in the United States of America, desiring them to adopt some measures for appointing a Grand Master over said States."

[...]

There were Grand Lodges in active existence in three of

the States at this time – viz., Massachusetts, Pennsylvania, and Virginia; and although the name of WASHINGTON for General Grand Master does not appear in the foregoing petition from the Masonic convention in the army, yet it was formally signified to these Grand Lodges that he was their choice. [...] Previous to the reception of the address of the Army Convention by the Grand Lodge of Pennsylvania, but while these proceedings were in progress, an emergent meeting of that grand body was convened at Philadelphia, on the 13th of January, 1780, to consider the propriety of appointing a General Grand Master over all the Grand Lodges formed or to be formed in the United States; and its records show, that:

"The ballot was put upon the question whether it be for the benefit of Masonry, that a GRAND MASTER of MASONS throughout the United States shall now be nominated on the part of this Grand Lodge; and it was unanimously determined in the affirmative.

Sundry respectable brethren being put in nomination, it was moved that the ballot be put for them separately, and his Excellency, GEORGE WASHINGTON, Esq., general and commander-in-chief of the army of the United States, being first in nomination, he was balloted for as Grand Master, and elected by unanimous vote of the whole lodge.

Ordered, that the minutes of this election and appointment must be transmitted to the different Grand Lodges in the United States, and their concurrence therein be requested, in order that application be made to his excellency in due form, praying that he will do the brethren and Craft the honor of accepting their appointment."

[...]

There is no doubt that in the minds of all his Masonic compeers, after the independence of this country was attained, he was justly regarded as the GREAT PATRON OF THE FRATERNITY IN AMERICA. [...] Nor was WASHINGTON'S fame as a Mason, or the belief that he was General Grand Master, confined to this country; for, in 1786, two letters in French were addressed to him, from Cape François, as *"Grand Master of America,"* soliciting a lodge-warrant for brethren on that island; which letters WASHINGTON caused to be laid before the Grand Lodge of Pennsylvania and they accordingly granted the warrant. A venerable brother in Virginia also informs us that his father, who was a Mason in Scotland, emigrated to this country soon after the close of the Revolutionary War; and that he had often heard him say that his Masonic brethren in Scotland congratulated him, when he left, on the advantages and protection he would enjoy from Masonry in this country, as General WASHINGTON they said was Grand Master of Masons here. This illusion was also perpetuated by a Masonic medal, which was struck in 1797, having on its obverse side the bust of WASHINGTON in military dress, with its legend, "G. WASHINGTON, PRESIDENT, 1797;" and on its reverse side, the emblems of Masonry, surrounded by the inscription, "AMOR, HONOR, ET JUSTICA," and the initials, "G.W., G. G. M."

Although the Grand Lodge of Pennsylvania did not succeed in creating a General Grand Mastership, and elevating WASHINGTON to that office, as was her desire, and also that of the Military Lodges of the army, from whom the proposition first sprang, yet that Grand Body still continued to regard him as first among American Masons. [...]

## Chapter V

[Washington almost becomes the head of another secret society]

[...] We have already noted in our sketch the strong desire of the Masonic brethren in the army that WASHINGTON should be constituted the head of Masons in this country. But as the time drew near, and no definite action of the whole Fraternity in America had been taken, an affectionate regard of the officers for their commander, and for each other, led them to form an association among themselves, having the social features of the Masonic institution as its leading principle, and designed, by inculcating benevolence and mutual relief, to perpetuate their friendships, and incite in their minds the most exalted patriotism. The idea of such a society is said to have originated with General KNOX, who communicated his plan to Baron STEUBEN; and at a general meeting of the officers, on the 13th of May, 1783, with the approbation of WASHINGTON, they instituted the "Society of the Cincinatti," and he became its first president, and continued to hold the office until his death. [...]

The newspapers of that period give an account of an earlier proposed association, or "New Order of American Knighthood," as it was called. As early as the 25th of March, 1783, the Philadelphia papers stated that,

"On the next anniversary of Independence, the 4th of July, a new Order of Knighthood, called the *Order of Freedom*, will be established, and the installation take place in the city of Philadelphia.

Patron of the Order;-St. Louis

Chief of the Order;- President of Congress for the time being.

Grand Master;- General WASHINGTON.

Chancellor;- Dr. FRANKLIN.

Prelate;- DR. WITHERSPOON.

Genealogist;- Mr. PAYNE.

Gentleman Usher;- Mr. THOMPSON.

Register and Secretary;- Mr. DIGGS.

Herald;- Mr. HUTCHINGS.

Twenty-four knight companions, consisting of the governor of each State for the time being, which they reckon nineteen.

General LINCOLN;- General GREENE;- General WAYNE;- Colonel LEE."

[...]

This we believe to have been the earliest attempt in the United States to form a social institution modelled after civic distinctions of society in Europe. Who its projectors were, who its advocates, and who its composers, we have not learned. Although such a society never went into existence, yet as it contemplated for General WASHINGTON the distinguished honor of being its Grand Master.

## Chapter VI

*[Washington is honoured by foreigners and members of his own lodge at Virginia]*

[...] In the autumn of 1784, LA FAYETTE came to America, and visited WASHINGTON at Mount Vernon. Of all the generals of the Revolution he had been the most beloved by WASHINGTON; and both to him and to his wife in France had the hospitalities of Mount Vernon been often tendered by Mr. and Mrs. WASHINGTON. Madame LA FAYETTE had wrought with her own hands in France a beautiful Masonic apron of white satin groundwork, with the emblems of Masonry delicately delineated with needle-work of colored silk; and this, with some other Masonic ornaments, was placed in a highly finished rose-wood box, also beautified with Masonic emblems, and brought to WASHINGTON on this occasion as a present by LA FAYETTE. It was a compliment to WASHINGTON and to Masonry delicately paid, and remained among the treasures of Mount Vernon till long after its recipient's death, when the apron was presented by his legatees to the Washington Benevolent Society, and by them to the Grand Lodge at Alexandria. The apron presented to WASHINGTON by Messrs. WATSON & CASSOUL two years before, and which is still in possession of

Lodge No. 22 at Alexandria, had been often mistaken for this; but the two aprons may be easily identified, by the WATSON & CASSOUL apron being wrought with gold and silver tissue, with the American and French flags combined upon it, while the LA FAYETTE apron is wrought with silk, and has for its design on the frontlet the Mark Master's circle, and mystic letters, with a *beehive* as its *mark* in the centre.

[...]

The following extract from the records of the Grand Lodge of Virginia shows its compliance with the request; and the memory of WASHINGTON as a Mason, and the first Master of this lodge under its Virginia charter had been prepared in this name.

"At a Grand Annual Communication of the Grand Lodge of Virginia begun and held in the Masons' Hall, in the city of Richmond, on the 9th day of December, Anno Lucis 5805, Anno Domini 1805.*

Whereas, at the last Grand Annual Communication a request was made by the Alexandria Lodge No. 22 for permission to change the name of the said Lodge to that of the Alexandria Washington Lodge, No. 22, which request was acceded and a new charter ordered to be issued; and whereas this order did not meet the wishes

---

*Editor's note: Anno Lucis, literally 'year of light', is based on a calendar that begins when God, according to the calculations of the medieval Archbishop Ussher, created the universe – for Adam is thought of as the first Freemason.

of the Brethren of the said Lodge, who having had our illustrious Brother General GEORGE WASHINGTON for their first Master, whose name is inserted as such in their original charter, they then were and still are desirous of preserving their said charter, as an honourable testimony of his regard for them and only wish to be permitted by the Grand Lodge to assume the name of the Alexandria Washington Lodge, No. 22, without changing their said charter therefor,

*Resolved*, That the said lodge be permitted to assume the said name, and that it be henceforth denominated the Alexandria Washington Lodge, No. 22."

## Chapter VII

[Washington is sworn in as President on a Masonic Bible and the corner-stone of Washington DC is laid according to Masonic rites]

WASHINGTON reached New York on the 23rd of April, and the 30th of the same month was the day fixed for his inauguration. On that occasion, General JACOB MORTON was marshal of the day. He was the Master of St. John's, the oldest lodge in the city, and at the same time Grand Secretary of the Grand Lodge of New York. General MORTON brought from the altar of his lodge the Bible with its cushion of crimson velvet, and upon that sacred volume, ROBERT R. LIVINGSTON, Chancellor of the State of New York, and Grand Master of its Grand Lodge, administered to WASHINGTON his oath of office as President of the United States.

Having taken the oath, WASHINGTON reverently bowed and kissed the sacred volume ; and the awful suspense of the moment was broken by Chancellor LIVINGSTON, who solemnly said, "Long Live GEORGE WASHINGTON, President of the United States!" A thousand tongues at once joined in repeated acclamations, "LONG LIVE GEORGE WASHINGTON!"

A memorial leaf of the sacred Book was then folded at the page on which WASHINGTON had devoutly impressed his lips; and the volume was returned to St. John's Lodge, and placed again upon its sacred altar.

A few years later it was again taken from its resting place, and borne in a solemn procession by the Masonic brethren of New York City, who met to pay funeral honors to the memory of WASHINGTON. It is still in possession of St. John's Lodge No. 1, who value it highly as a sacred memento. The memory of WASHINGTON'S oath of office upon it is perpetuated by [an] inscription, beautifully engrossed, and accompanied by a miniature likeness from an engraving by LENEY, which were inserted by order of the lodge.

[...]

During his absence, [WASHINGTON'S] lodge at Alexandria had performed a public labor, in the ceremonials of erecting the first corner-stone of the District of Columbia near that city. As this Federal territory was required, by an act of Congress, to embrace a district of country ten miles square, lying on both sides of the Potomac,

WASHINGTON had appointed commissioners to establish its boundaries, and its *south-east* corner-stone was set with Masonic ceremonies on the 15th of April, 1791. Its location was at Jones' Point near the mouth of Hunting Creek, on the bank of the Potomac, near where the Lighthouse at Alexandria now stands.

[...]

[Washington DC] was at first called "The Federal City," and WASHINGTON thus styled it in a letter written on the 13th of April 1791; but the commissioners appointed to superintend the laying out of the city had employed Major L'ENFANT, a French architect, to form plans and drawings of it; and in a letter to him, bearing the date of the 9th September, 1791, they informed him that they had agreed that the Federal District should be called "The Territory of Columbia," and the Federal City, "The City of Washington," and directed him to thus designate them on his maps.

## Chapter VIII

[Washington himself lays the corner-stone of the Capitol Building wearing his Masonic apron]

[...] On the 18th of September of [1793], WASHINGTON laid the corner-stone of the Capitol of the United States, in the city that bore his name. It was laid at the *southeast* corner of the edifice, it being the custom of our Masonic fathers to place it at that point, and not at the *northeast* as at present. The following account of the

ceremonies on the occasion was published in the news-papers of that day.

"GEORGETOWN, September 21, 1793.

On Wednesday one of the grandest Masonic processions took place, for the purpose of laying the corner-stone of the Capitol of the United States, which, perhaps, was ever exhibited on the like important occasion. About ten o'clock, Lodge No. 9 was visited by that congregation so graceful to the Craft, Lodge No. 22 of Virginia, with all their officers and regalia; and directly afterwards appeared on the southern banks of the grand river Potomac, one of the finest companies of volunteer artillery that hath been lately seen, parading to receive the President of the United States, who shortly came in sight with his suit, to whom the artillery paid their military honors; and his Excellency and suit crossed the Potomac, and was received in Maryland by the officers and brethren of No. 22 Virginia, and No. 9 Maryland, whom the

President headed, preceded by a band of music; the rear brought up by the Alexandria volunteer artillery, with grand solemnity of march, proceeded to the President's square, in the city of Washington, where they were met and saluted by No. 15 of the City of Washington in all their elegant badges and clothing, headed by Brother JOSEPH CLARK, Rt. W.G.M., P.T., and conducted to a large lodge prepared for the purpose of their reception. After a short space of time, by the vigilance of Brother CLOTWORTHY STEPHENSON, Grand Marshal P.T., the brotherhood and other bodies were disposed in a second order of procession, which took place amidst a brilliant crowd of spectators of both sexes.

[...]

"The President of the United States and his attendant brethren ascended from the cavazion to the east of the corner-stone; and there Grand Master P.T., elevated on a triple rostrum, delivered an oration fitting the occasion, which was received with brotherly love and commendation. At intervals, during the delivery of the oration, several volleys were discharged by the artillery. The ceremony ended in prayer, Masonic chanting honors, and a 15-volley from the artillery."

WASHINGTON, although holding at this time no official rank in Masonry, except that of Past Master of Lodge No. 22, at Alexandria, clothed himself for the occasion with an apron and other insignia of a Mason, and, as the foregoing account shows, was honoured with the chief place in the procession and ceremonies. [...] No act of WASHINGTON was more historic than this, and yet it has found no place on the pages of our country's history. It was he who first in the hearts of all men, honouring Masonry by his presence as a brother, and sanctioning by his participation as the chief actor in its highest public ceremonies, dignified its claims as an institution worthy of national confidence and regard. And yet the compilers of our country's annals have ignored the fact, or left it unrecorded on their pages, until their silence has been made to testify that WASHINGTON disdained to publicly avow himself a Mason. But he stood on that occasion before his brethren and the world as the representative of SOLOMON of old, who, the Jewish historian says, "laid the foundation of the Temple very deep in the ground; and the materials were strong stones, and such as would resist the force of time." Those who would blot the record of the mystic labors of WASHINGTON would blush at the memory of one wiser than he.

[...]

This portrait was placed in an elegant gilt frame, and hung upon the walls of the lodge-room. Its collar and jewel are those of a Past Master, a rank which WASHINGTON held in his lodge; and its sash and apron represent those presented to him by Messrs. WATSON & CASSOUL.

## Chapter IX

[Washington receives letters from high-profile Masons]

[...] "The *East*, the *West*, and the *South*, of the Grand Lodge of Ancient Free and Accepted Masons, for the Commonwealth of Massachusetts, to their most worthy Brother GEORGE WASHINGTON.

Wishing ever to be foremost in testimonials of respect and admiration of those virtues and services with which you have so long adorned and benefited our common country, and not the last nor least to regret the cessation of them in the public councils of the Union; your brethren of this Grand Lodge embrace the earliest opportunity of greeting you in the calm retirement you have contemplated to yourself.

Though as citizens they lose you in the active labors of political life, they hope as Masons to find you in the pleasing sphere of fraternal engagement. From the cares of State, and the fatigues of public business, our institution opens a recess, affording all the relief of tranquillity, the harmony of peace, and the refreshment of pleasure. Of these may you partake in all their purity and satisfaction; and we will assure ourselves that your attachment to this social plan will encrease; and that, under the auspices of your encouragement, assistance, and patronage, the Craft will attain its highest ornament, perfection, and praise. And it is our earnest prayer that when your light shall be no more visible in this earthly Temple, you may be raised to the *All Perfect Lodge* above, be seated on the right of the Supreme Architect of the Universe, and receive the refreshment your labors have merited.

On behalf of the Grand Lodge, we subscribe ourselves, with the highest esteem, your affectionate brethren,

PAUL REVERE, Grand Master.
ISAIAH THOMAS, Senior Grand Warden.
JOSEPH LAUGHTON, Junior Grand Warden.
DANIEL OLIVER, Grand Secretary.
BOSTON, March 21, 5797."

To this address WASHINGTON returned the following

reply, which was communicated to the Grand Lodge on the 12th of the following June:

"TO THE GRAND LODGE OF ANCIENT FREE AND ACCEPTED MASONS IN THE COMMONWEALTH OF MASSACHUSETTS:

"BROTHERS – it was not until within these few days that I have been favored by the receipt of your affectionate address, dated in Boston, the 21st March.

"For the favorable sentiments you have been pleased to express on the occasion of my past services, and for the regrets with which they are accompanied for the cessation of my public functions, I pray you to accept my best acknowledgments and gratitude.

"No pleasure, except that which results from a consciousness of having, to the utmost of my abilities, discharged the trusts which have been reposed in me by my country, can equal the satisfaction I feel for the unequivocal proofs I continually receive of its approbation of my public conduct; and I beg you to be assured that the evidence thereof, which is exhibited by the Grand Lodge of Massachusetts, is not among the least pleasing or grateful to my feelings.

"In that retirement which declining years induces me to seek, and which repose, to a mind long employed in public concerns, rendered necessary, my wishes that bounteous Providence will continue to bless and preserve our country in peace, and in the prosperity it has enjoyed, will be warm and sincere; and my attachment to the Society of which we are members will dispose me always to contribute my best endeavors to promote the honor and interest of the Craft.

"For the prayer you offer on my behalf, I entreat you to accept the thanks of a grateful heart, with assurances of fraternal regard, and my best wishes for the honor, happiness, and prosperity of all the members of the Grand Lodge of Massachusetts."

### Chapter X

[Washington is taken ill, dies, and is buried according to Masonic funeral rites]

WASHINGTON'S last summer and autumn were spent in arranging the minutest details of his domestic affairs and private business. Whether he had a premonition that it was his last year, no one can determine; but like a wise man, he set his house in order. December came, and with its chilling breath and wintry mantle came also the messenger of death for WASHINGTON!

His sickness was sudden, short, and painful. It commenced on the evening of Thursday, the 12th of December, as a common cold, with soreness of the throat. Upon the succeeding day the inflammation there had increased, and in the night became alarming. He was urged to send to Alexandria for Dr. CRAIK, his family physician, but the night was stormy, and his humanity for his servant induced him to defer it until Saturday morning, using, in the mean time, all the usual domestic remedies in such cases. But these were of no avail, and his physicians came too late. It was eleven o'clock on the forenoon of Saturday before Dr. CRAIK arrived, and the disease had made so alarming a progress that two eminent consulting physicians, Dr. DICK, of Alexandria, and Dr. BROWN, of Port Tobacco, were also sent for. But none of them could afford relief. The chilling hand of death was already upon him. Fully aware that his last mortal hour had come, he met it with a composure of mind that astonished those about him, saying to his physician, who assured him that he had not long to live: "It is well, doctor: I am not afraid to die." Then calmly crossing his arms upon his breast, he closed his eyes, and, with a few shortening breaths, expired without a struggle, between ten and eleven in the evening. […]

Few were present as witnesses of the scene. It was only the domestic circle of his own household, with, perhaps, a few family friends, and his attending physicians who were there. Of these, Dr. CRAIK, his life-long friend and family physician, and Dr. DICK, were Masons; the latter being at the time the Master of WASHINGTON'S own lodge at Alexandria. What Masonic requests may have been made to them during his last hours we know not. But it is well known to every Mason that the mystic rites of a Masonic burial are not performed, except at a brother's request while living, or by desire of his family after his death. It was believed at the time, by intelligent brethren, that WASHINGTON had signified that to be his wish; and the holy rites of the Christian Church of which he was a member, and the mystic rites of Masonry, were each performed in their beautiful simplicity at the tomb of this distinguished brother.

At midnight – *the low twelve of Masonry* – the body was taken from the chamber of death to a large drawing-room below, clothed in burial robes. The death dew had been wiped from its brow, and the pale taper at its head threw a flickering light on the marble features where death had set his signet. From midnight until morning there was stillness there. Words were spoken only in whispers, as if accents from human lips would fall discordant on the sleeper's ear. America, too, in that dread interval from midnight to Sabbath morn lay in slumber, unconscious of her loss. Morning came, and the hurrying footsteps of family friends, who hastened to Mount Vernon, were heard mingling with those that left to carry the tidings of a Nation's loss! My pen cannot describe what followed. A pencil painted it:

"During the day a plain mahogany coffin was ordered from Alexandria, and mourning for the family, overseers, and domestics at Mount Vernon. The funeral was appointed for Wednesday, the 18th, at meridian; and the Rev. Mr. DAVIS, the Episcopal clergyman at Alexandria, was invited to perform the burial rites of that Church on the occasion. The selection was an appropriate one; for Mr. DAVIS was not only the rector of WASHINGTON'S church, but he was also a member of the same Masonic lodge.

"The funeral procession and burial ceremonies were

arranged by a committee of Lodge No. 22, at Alexandria, consisting of Dr. ELISHA CULLEN DICK, its Master; Colonel GEORGE DENEALE, its Senior Warden; and Colonels CHARLES LITTLE and CHARLES SIMMS, who were members. On Monday, the 16th, an emergent meeting of this lodge was called, at which Dr. DICK, its Master, presided. Forty-one of its members were present, and two visiting brethren, one from Fredericksburg, where WASHINGTON was made a Mason, and the other from Philadelphia. [...]

"The sun had passed its meridian height before the Fraternity and military escort arrived from Alexandria. The Masonic apron and two crossed swords were then placed upon the coffin, a few mystic words were spoken, and the brethren one by one filed by the noble form, majestic even in death, and took a last sad look on one they had loved so well. Alas, the light of his eye and the breathing of his lips in language of fraternal greeting were lost to them forever on this side of the grave! [...]

"The Rev. Mr. DAVIS broke the silence by repeating from sacred writings, 'I am the resurrection and the life; he that believeth in Me, though he were dead, yet shall he live.' Then with bowed and reverent heads all listened to the voice of prayer; and as the holy words went on, as used in the beautiful and expressive burial-service of the Episcopal Church, their soothing spirit was echoed in the responses of the multitude around. Mr. DAVIS closed his burial-service with a short address. There was a pause; and then the Master of the lodge performed the mystic funeral rites of Masonry, as the last service at the burial of WASHINGTON. The apron and the swords were removed from the coffin, for their place was no longer there. It was ready for entombment. The brethren one by one cast upon it an evergreen sprig; and their hearts spoke the Mason's farewell as they bestowed their last mystic gift. There was a breathless silence there during this scene. So still was all around in the gathered multitude of citizens, that they might almost have heard the echoes of the acacia as it fell with trembling lightness upon the coffin-lid. The pall-bearers placed their precious burden in the tomb's cold embrace, earth was cast on the threshold, and the words were spoken: '*Earth to earth – ashes to ashes – dust to dust!*' and the entombment of WASHINGTON was finished. The mystic public burial honors of Masonry were given by each brother with lifted hands, saying in his heart, 'Alas! my Brother! *we have knelt with thee in prayer, we have pressed thee to our bosoms, we will meet thee in heaven!*' The mystic chain was reunited in the circle there, the cannon on the vessel and on the banks above them fired their burial salute, and Mount Vernon's tomb was left in possession of its noblest sleeper. The sun was then setting, and the pall of night mantled the pathway of the Masonic brethren as they sadly returned to their homes."

## WASHINGTON IN HIS OWN WORDS

George Washington received a large number of letters from his Masonic brethren and would often take the time to write detailed replies:

To George Washington, *President of the United States*:
Sir and Brother – The Ancient York Masons of the jurisdiction of Pennsylvania, for the first time assembled in General Communication to celebrate the feast of St. John the Evangelist since your election to the chair of government of the United States, beg leave to approach you with congratulations from the East, and, in the pride of fraternal affection, to hail you as the great master-builder (under the Supreme Architect), by whose labors the temple of liberty hath been reared in the West, exhibiting to the nations of the earth a model of beauty, order, and harmony, worthy of their imitation and praise.

Your knowledge of the origin and objects of our institution – its tendency to promote the social affections and harmonize the heart – give us a sure pledge that this tribute of our veneration, this effusion of love, will not be ungrateful to you; nor will Heaven reject our prayer, that you may be long continued to adorn the bright list of master workmen which our Fraternity produces in the terrestrial lodge; and that you may be late removed to that celestial lodge where love and harmony reign transcendent and divine; where the Great Architect more immediately presides, and where cherubim and seraphim wafting our congratulations from earth to heaven shall hail you brother!

By order and on behalf of the Grand Lodge of Pennsylvania, in General Communication assembled in ample form.

J.B. Smith, G.M.

*To the Ancient York Masons of the Jurisdiction of Pennsylvania:*

I receive your kind congratulations with the purest sensations of fraternal affection; and from a heart deeply impressed with your generous wishes for my present and future happiness, I beg you to accept my thanks. -- At the same time, I request you will be assured of my best wishes and earnest prayers for your happiness while you remain in this terrestrial mansion and that we may hereafter meet as brethren in the eternal Temple of the Supreme Architect.

G. Washington

*To their honored and Illustrious Brother -- George Washington. December 27, 1792*

Whilst the Historian is describing the career of your glory, and the inhabitants of an extensive Empire are made happy in your unexampled exertions:-- whilst some celebrate the Hero so distinguished in liberating United America and others the Patriot who presides over her Councils, a band of brothers having always joined the acclamations of their Countrymen now intensify their respect for those milder virtues which have ever graced the man.

Taught by the precepts of our Society, that all its members stand upon a level, we venture to assume this station and to approach you with that freedom which diminishes our differences without lessening our respect. Desirous to enlarge the boundaries of our social happiness, and to vindicate the ceremonies of their institution, this Grand Lodge have published a "Book of Constitutions," (and a copy for your acceptance accompanies this) which by discovering the principles that actuate will speak the Eulogy of the Society; though they fervently wish the conduct of its members may prove its higher commendation.

Convinced of his attachment to its cause, and readiness to encourage its benevolent designs; they have taken the liberty to dedicate this work to one, the qualities of whose heart and the actions of whole life have contributed to improve personal virtue, and extend throughout the world the most endearing cordialities, and they humbly hope he will pardon this freedom and accept the tribute of their esteem & homage. May the Supreme Architect of the Universe bless and protect you -- give you length of days & increase of felicity in this world, and then receive you to the harmonious and exalted city in Heaven.

John Cutter, Grand Master

Josiah Bartlett, Munso Mackey – Grand Wardens
Boston
Decem. 27. A.D. 1772.

*Letter from George Washington to Massachusetts Masons Grand Lodge, December 27, 1792. (Appreciation for the honor, dedication and gift of Book of Constitutions)*

To the Grand Master of the Free & Accepted Masons, for the Commonwealth of Massachusetts.

Flattering as it may be to the human mind, & truly honorable as it is to receive from our fellow citizens testimonies of approbation for exertions to promote the public welfare; it is not less pleasing to know that the milder virtues of the heart are highly respected by a society whose liberal principles must be founded in the immediate laws of truth and justice. To enlarge the sphere of social happiness is worthy the benevolent design of the Masonic Institution; and it is most fervently to be wished that the conduct of every member of the fraternity, as well as those publications which discover the principles which actuate them, may tend to convince Mankind that the grand object of Masonry is to promote the happiness of the human race.

While I beg your acceptance of my thanks for the "Book of Constitutions" you have sent me, and the honor you have done me in the dedication, permit me to assure you that I feel all those emotions of gratitude which your affectionate address & cordial wishes are calculated to inspire: and I sincerely pray that the Great Architect of the Universe may bless you and receive you hereafter into his immortal Temple.

G. Washington

*To George Washington, from George Washington Snyder
of Fredericktown, Maryland, August 23, 1798*

"Sir – You will, I hope, not think it presumption in a
stranger, whose name, perhaps, never reached your ears,
to address himself to you, the commanding general of a
great nation. I am a German born, and liberally educated
in the city of Heidelberg, in the Palatinate of the Rhine.
I came to this country in 1776, and felt soon after my
arrival a close attachment to the liberty for which these
Confederated States then struggled. The same attachment
still remains, not glowing, but burning in my breast. At
the same time that I am exulting in the measures adopted
by our Government, I feel myself elevated in the idea of
my adopted country. I am attached, both from the best
of education and mature inquiry and research, to the
simple doctrines of Christianity, which I have the honor
to teach in public; and I do heartily despise all the cavils
of infidelity. Our present time is pregnant with the most
shocking evils and calamities, which threaten ruin to our
liberty and Government. Secretly the most secret plans
are in agitation; plans calculated to ensnare the unwary,
to attract the gay and irreligious, and to entice even the
well-disposed to combine in the general machine for
overturning all government and religion.

It was some time since that a book fell into my hands,
entitled "Proofs of a Conspiracy, etc., by John Robison,"
which gives a full account of a Society of Freemasons that
distinguishes itself by the name of "Illuminati," whose

plan is to overturn all government and all religion, even natural, and who endeavour to eradicate every idea of a Supreme Being, and distinguish man from beast by his shape only.

A thought suggested itself to me that some of the lodges in the United States might have caught the infection, and might co-operate with the Illuminate, or the Jacobine clubs in France. [...]

Your Excellency's

Very humble and devoted servant,

G.W. Snyder

Fredericktown, Maryland, August 23, 1798

### Letter of George Washington to George Washington Snyder, September 25, 1798

Sir: Many apologies are due to you, for my not acknowledging the receipt of your obliging favor of the 22d. Ulto, and for not thanking you, at an earlier period, for the Book you had the goodness to send me.

I have heard much of the nefarious and dangerous plan, and doctrines of the Illuminati, but never saw the Book until you were pleased to send it to me. The same causes which have prevented my acknowledging the receipt of your letter have prevented my reading the Book, hitherto; namely, the multiplicity of matters which pressed upon me before, and the debilitated state in which I was left after, a severe fever had been removed. And which allows me to add little more now, than thanks for your kind wishes and favourable sentiments, except to correct an error you have run into, of my Presiding over the English lodges in this Country. The fact is, I preside over none, nor have I been in one more than once or twice, within the last thirty years. I believe notwithstanding, that none of the Lodges in this Country are contaminated with the principles ascribed to the Society of the Illuminati. With respect I am &c.

[George Snyder wrote another letter in the same vein, to which Washington made the following reply:]

### Letter of George Washington to George Washington Snyder, October 24, 1798

Revd Sir: I have your favor of the 17th. instant before me; and my only motive to trouble you with the receipt of this letter is to explain, and correct a mistake which I perceive the hurry in which I am obliged, often, to write letters, have led you into.

It was not my intention to doubt that the Doctrines of the Illuminati, and principles of Jacobinism had not spread in the United States. On the contrary, no one is more truly satisfied of this fact than I am.

The idea that I meant to convey, was, that I did not believe that the Lodges of Free Masons in this Country had, as Societies, endeavoured to propagate the diabolical tenets of the first, or pernicious principles of the latter (if they are susceptible of separation). That individuals of them may have done it, or that the founder, or instrument employed to found, the Democratic Societies in the United States, may have had these objects; and actually had a separation of the People from their Government in view, is too evident to be questioned.

My occupations are such that but little leisure is allowed me to read News Papers, or Books of any kind; the reading of letters, and preparing answers, absorb much of my time. With respect, etc.

*To George Washington, Most Respected Brother:*

The Ancient York Masons of Lodge No. 22 offer you their warmest congratulations, on your retirement from your useful labours. Under the Supreme Architect of the Universe, you have been the Master Workman in erecting the Temple of Liberty in the West, on the broad basis of equal rights. In your wise administration of the Government of the United States for the space of eight years, you have kept within the compass of our happy constitutions, and acted upon the square with foreign nations, and thereby preserved your country in peace, and promoted the prosperity and happiness of your fellow-citizens. And now that you have returned from the labors of public life, to the refreshment of domestic tranquillity, they ardently pray that you may long enjoy all the happiness which the Terrestrial Lodge can afford, and finally be received to a

Celestial lodge, where love, peace, and harmony forever reign, and cherubim and seraphim shall hail you Brother!

By the unanimous desire of Lodge No. 22

James Gillis, Master

April 4, 1797

*Letter of George Washington to the Brothers of the Ancient York Masons No. 22*

While my heart acknowledges with brotherly love your affectionate congratulations on my retirement from the arduous toils of past years, my gratitude is no less excited by your kind wishes for my future happiness. If it has pleased the Supreme Architect of the Universe to make me an humble instrument to promote the welfare and happiness of my fellow-men, my exertions have been abundantly recompensed by the kind partiality with which they have been received. And the assurances you give me of your belief that I have acted upon the square in my public capacity, will be among my principal enjoyments in this Terrestrial Lodge.

George Washington

## ◆ CHAPTER IV ◆

# Masonry in the USA:
# Two Major Myths

onspiracy theorists have an unshakeable belief that the Freemasons, along with another society that has its roots in Freemasonry, the Illuminati (see Chapter VI), have long been in control of the US government. One apparent proof of this is that the streets of Washington DC were supposedly planned to form symbols associated with Freemasonry; another is the presence of the allegedly Masonic emblems on the Great Seal which can be seen on the back of the dollar bill.

## THE MASONIC LAYOUT OF WASHINGTON DC

In *The Lost Symbol*, Dan Brown mentions the conspiracy theory that pentagrams and other esoteric symbols can be seen in the layout of the streets of Washington DC.

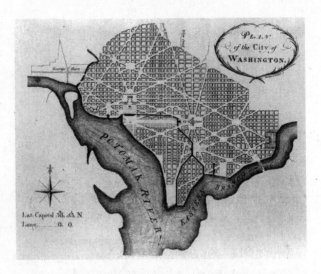

*Pierre L'Enfant's plan of the city of Washington*

While Brown reveals the Masonic significance behind the Washington Monument, for which records show many Masonic lodges contributed stones, his character Robert Langdon dismisses the notion of a Masonic significance behind the city's layout as complete nonsense. Let's look at the facts.

Pierre L'Enfant, who designed the original street layout of the nation's capital in 1791, was not a Freemason. His original design can be seen above, and, although it does include a number of central squares from which diagonal roads emanate, it does not show any obvious pentagrams

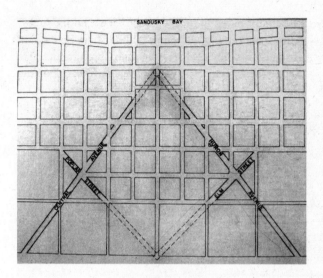

*Map of Sandusky, Ohio*

(five-pointed stars), Seals of Solomon (Stars of David) or the Square and Compasses that some maintain are built into the streets of DC.

Similarly, the suggestions that the Pentagon really forms part of a pentagram is not backed up by any evidence, nor is the even more far-fetched idea that the two large diagonal streets that flank the Mall form the tip of a figure of Baphomet, with the Capitol Building as the head of the goat-human demigod (see 'A Masonic Hoax' in Chapter II) and the two lawns at the back of the Capitol building forming Baphomet's horns. Imaginative though these ideas may be, they have no basis in fact and can safely be dismissed as myths, although this hasn't stopped authors from writing entire books on the symbols that can allegedly be found in the streets of DC.

However, a little-known fact is that there *is* a city in the US which was deliberately laid out in the form of Masonic symbols – Sandusky, Ohio. The streets of the city form the three Great Lights of Masonry: The Volume of the Sacred Law, over which are laid the set square and the pair of compasses. The central North–South street (not named on the diagram on page 189, but in fact Columbus Avenue), forms the spine of the book, while Poplar Street and Elm Street form the set square and Central Avenue and Huron Avenue form the compasses.

## THE GREAT SEAL

The speculation over the Masonic symbols allegedly visible in the Great Seal of the United States, which is shown on the back of the American dollar bill, does have some basis in fact.

Benjamin Franklin, who, as we know, wrote the first Masonic book to be printed in America and was a Grand Master of the Pennsylvania Masonic Lodge, was a member of the first committee that was petitioned by Congress on the first day of Independence of the United States, 4 July 1776, to 'bring in a device for a seal for the United States

*The Great Seal of the United States (obverse)*

*The Great Seal of the United States (reverse)*

of America'. Alongside Franklin, the committee consisted of John Adams, who spoke favourably of Freemasonry but never joined, and Thomas Jefferson, who was also not himself a Mason, but was a Masonic sympathiser.

This first committee initially tried to design the seal themselves, but after unsuccessfully attempting to incorporate various Biblical and Classical themes, including Franklin's suggestion, which depicted Moses (or 'Grand Master Moses' as Franklin wrote of him in his *Constitutions*) overwhelming Pharaoh, they enlisted the help of the artist and heraldic expert, Pierre Eugene du Simitiere.

Du Simitiere submitted his design (opposite), drawn up under the guidance of Adams, Jefferson and Franklin, on 20 August 1776. The Frenchman's design was much more conventional than any of the previous versions, but it was not accepted by Congress.

Note that the infamous Masonic symbol, the Eye of Providence, became part of the Great Seal at this early stage, when Franklin still had direct influence on the Seal's design. This symbol, originally of Egyptian origin (as the Eye of Horus), was one of the symbols used by the Masons to signify The Great Architect of the Universe, although it was not particularly common at the time.

A second committee was formed, whose design, consisting of a flag of 13 red and white stripes in a heraldic shield flanked by a figure holding an olive branch and a Native American warrior with a bow and arrow, above

*Pierre du Simitiere's rejected design for the Great Seal*

which shone 13 stars surrounded by clouds, was also rejected by Congress.

A third committee's design introduced the symbol of the 13-step unfinished pyramid, which had already been used as a symbol on currency by John Hopkinson – a man who some Masonic authorities claim as one of their own and who was directly involved in producing the second committee's design for the Great Seal. The pyramid represented the great, but unfinished, work of building America. The third committee also brought in the emblem of the eagle, which was initially not the American bald eagle, but a smaller bird.

But Congress did not approve this design either. Instead the Secretary of Congress, Charles Thomson, took it upon himself to do the work and combined various elements from the earlier designs into a single piece, which formed the basis of the Great Seal that we know today. He wrote the following explanation of the symbols upon the occasion of the design's being adopted on 20 June 1782:

'The Escutcheon is composed of the chief & pale, the two most honorable ordinaries. The Pieces, paly, represent the several states all joined in one solid compact entire, supporting a Chief, which unites the whole & represents Congress. The Motto alludes to this union. The pales in the arms are kept closely united by the chief and the Chief depends upon that union & the strength resulting from it for its support, to denote the Confederacy of the United States of America & the preservation of their union through Congress.

'The colours of the pales are those used in the flag of the United States of America; White signifies purity and innocence, Red, hardiness & valor, and Blue, the colour of the Chief signifies vigilance, perseverance & justice. The Olive branch and arrows denote the power of peace & war which is exclusively vested in Congress. The Constellation denotes a new State taking its place and rank among other sovereign powers. The Escutcheon is born on the breast of an American Eagle without any other supporters to denote that the United States of America ought to rely on their own Virtue.

'Reverse. The pyramid signifies Strength and Duration: The Eye over it & the Motto allude to the many signal interpositions of providence in favour of the American cause. The date underneath is that of the Declaration of Independence and the words under it signify the beginning of the new American Æra, which commences from that date.'

Conspiracy theorists have seen particular significance in several elements of the Seal:

- The pyramid and the Eye of Providence on the reverse side – both reminiscent of the Egyptian symbols used in Freemasonry.
- The stars above the eagle on the obverse side – these form a Seal of Solomon (also known as a Star of David), a central Masonic symbol.
- The motto *Novus ordo seclorum* – often mistranslated as 'A new world order' or even 'A new secular order' (as in Dan Brown's *Angels and Demons*), this motto should be translated as 'A new order of the ages', signifying the new era that American independence had ushered in.
- The number thirteen – there are many instances of the number thirteen on both sides of the seal: there are thirteen letters in each of the mottos *E pluribus unum* ('From the many, one') and *Annuit coeptis* ('He [God] has favoured our undertakings'); there are thirteen stars in the Seal of Solomon above the eagle's head; there are thirteen stripes on the shield on the reverse side; the eagle carries thirteen arrows and an olive branch with thirteen leaves and thirteen olives; there are thirteen steps in the pyramid. Many have seen this as a connection to the Masons, for whom 1, 3 and 13 are sacred numbers, but the prevalence of the number thirteen is in fact intended to commemorate the thirteen original states of the USA.

- The date: MDCCLXXVI (1776) – which conspiracy theorists suggest really commemorates the founding of the Illuminati by Adam Weishaupt (see Chapter VI), rather than the independence of the United States of America.

So, despite the connection with Benjamin Franklin and other Masonic sympathisers, it seems as if the Great Seal of the United States does not in fact deal in Masonic symbols. However, the decision to print the seal on the one-dollar bill is not unsuspicious, as it was taken in 1935 by known Mason Franklin D. Roosevelt and his fellow Masonic brother, Secretary of Agriculture Henry A. Wallace. Wallace convinced Roosevelt to include the Seal on the back of the dollar note, suggesting that the phrase *Novus ordo seclorum* seemed to echo Roosevelt's

'New Deal'. Dan Brown mentions this in *Angels and Demons*, but unfortunately is inaccurate when he suggests that Roosevelt did not let anyone else view the seal before submitting it. As the document opposite shows, Roosevelt was one of many men who approved the seal. However, it was only Roosevelt who asked that the obverse and reverse side of the seal be swapped around (compare the version shown here with a real dollar note) – ostensibly in order that his captions 'The Great Seal' 'of the United States' read left to right. Or might there have been another motive behind this seemingly innocuous act?

# • CHAPTER V •

# The 33 Degrees

he initiation rituals of the three degrees of 'Blue Lodge Masonry' have already been described in Chapter I, but in Dan Brown's *The Lost Symbol*, many of the characters are described as '33rd degree' Masons. These extra degrees are part of one of the major strands of Masonic tradition (officially known as 'Masonic Appendant Bodies') called the 'Scottish Rite'. Technically, these extra degrees are not superior to the rank of Master Masons and are meant merely to 'enrich' the philosophy of the Blue Lodge. Candidates must be invited to join the 33rd degree, entitled 'Sovereign Grand Inspector General'. They must be at least 33 years of age, already be 32nd degree Masons, and their numbers are restricted: in England there can only be 75 of these 33rd degree Masons at any one time. Each of the extra degrees of the Scottish

Rite is conferred singly in the USA (whereas many are conferred in name only in UK Scottish Rite lodges) and each is accompanied by an allegorical ceremony, which contains a specific lesson that the Mason must learn in order to rise up the ranks.

## THE 33 DEGREES OF SCOTTISH RITE FREEMASONRY

**1° *Entered Apprentice***
This degree begins a man's journey into freemasonry and represents youth.

**2° *Fellowcraft***
This degree symbolises man in adulthood and represents work.

**3° *Master Mason***
This degree represents man in old age and relates to wisdom.

**4° *Secret Master***
In this degree, the dignity of fidelity and integrity is demonstrated.

### 5° *Perfect Master*
This degree teaches that unworthy ambitions are corruptive and destructive to the man who forgets his duty to family, country and God.

### 6° *Intimate Secretary*
This degree shows that a man who is trustworthy can survive false accusations.

### 7° *Provost and Judge*
This degree teaches that Truth prevails, and Justice triumphs, tempered with mercy and forgiveness.

### 8° *Intendant of the Building*
This degree symbolises that the personal goal of title and position can cause strife.

### 9° *Master Elect of Nine*
This degree teaches that Truth often emerges from the clash of opinions, and to look at life and duty and God through the minds of others who do not share the same religious faith.

### 10° *Master Elect of Fifteen*
This degree uses the symbolism of Solomon's life and teaches how his pride prevented him from asking for forgiveness.

## 11° *Sublime Master Elected*

This degree emphasises virtue of good citizenship and teaches that a man should ever be loyal, brave and courageous in the conviction that right will eventually prevail.

## 12° *Grand Master Architect*

This degree teaches that the quality of Mercy through a spirit of compassion and a tenderness of heart will enable one to overlook injuries, or to treat the offender better than they deserve.

## 13° *Master of the Ninth Arch*

This degree portrays the history and legend of Enoch and prepares the candidate for the 14th degree.

## 14° *Grand Elect Mason*

This degree describes the constant endeavour of perfection of character.

## 15° *Knight of the East or Sword*

This degree shows the important lesson by the example of Zerubbabel, of loyalty to conviction, fidelity to duty, and devotion to Truth.

## 16° *Prince of Jerusalem*

This degree is a drama of the rewards found in the lessons of the 15th degree.

### 17° *Knight of the East and West*
This degree teaches that one should learn from, and avoid repeating, the errors of the past.

### 18° *Knight of the Rose Croix of H.R.D.M.*
This degree affirms the principles of tolerance and grants to each man the right to answer, in his own way, his convictions.

### 19° *Grand Pontiff*
This degree proclaims the spiritual unity of all who believe in God and cherish the hope of immortality, no matter what religious leader they follow or what creed they profess. It is concerned primarily with the perennial conflict between light and darkness, good and evil, God and Satan.

### 20° *Master ad Vitam*
This degree is a drama of the American spirit confronting the challenge of disloyalty and treason. Masonic principles and leadership are subjected to a crucial test. The degree demonstrates the Masonic condemnation of all who conspire against the security of the nation and the happiness of our people.

### 21° *Patriarch Noachite*
This degree teaches that Freemasonry is not a shield for evil doing and that justice is one of the chief supports of the fraternity.

### 22° *Prince of Libanus*
In this degree, the dignity of labour is demonstrated. It is no curse, but a privilege, for man to be allowed to earn his sustenance by work. Idleness, not labour, is disgraceful.

### 23° *Chief of the Tabernacle*
This degree teaches that those with faith in God and love for their fellow man will make great sacrifices to help others.

### 24° *Prince of the Tabernacle*
This degree teaches that a mutual belief in a Supreme Power should bind all men together in a world-wide brotherhood.

### 25° *Knight of the Brazen Serpent*
This degree teaches that there are desert stretches in every individual life in the history of every nation, with a resultant breakdown of discipline and loss of faith. This degree is a clarion call to faith in ourselves, in each other, and in God.

### 26° *Prince of Mercy*
This degree teaches the quality of mercy; that it is a spirit of compassion and a tenderness of heart which dispose us to overlook injuries and to treat an offender better than he deserves.

### 27° *Commander of the Temple*

This degree teaches that Scottish Rite Freemasonry believes in the concept of a free church in a free state, each supreme in its own sphere, neither seeking to dominate the other, but cooperating for the common good.

### 28° *Knight of the Sun*

This degree using the symbolism of the tools and implements of architecture teaches that by building high moral character among its adherents, Freemasonry may advance man's determined quest for the achievement of unity and good will throughout the world.

### 29° *Knight of St Andrew*

This degree emphasises the Masonic teachings of equality and toleration. We are reminded that no one man, no one Church, no one religion, has a monopoly of truth; that while we must be true and faithful to our own convictions, we must respect the opinions of others.

### 30° *Grand Elect Knight Kadosh*

This degree sets forth the tests and ceremonies that symbolise the experiences we must undergo in the building of excellence in character.

### 31° *Grand Inspector Inquisitor Commander*

This degree teaches that we should give every man the benefit of innocence and purity of intentions. He who would judge others must first judge himself.

### 32° *Sublime Prince of the Royal Secret*

This degree describes the victory of the spiritual over the human in man and the conquest of appetites and passions by moral sense and reason. The exemplar represents every Freemason eager to serve humanity but caught between self-interest and the call of duty. Duty often requires sacrifice, sometimes the supreme sacrifice.

### 33° *Sovereign Grand Inspector General*

This degree is conferred by the Supreme Council upon Freemasons of the 32nd degree in recognition of distinguished Masonic or public service. It cannot be applied for, but is conferred by invitation only. It is widely believed that 'all is revealed at the 33rd degree', but Masons jealously guard the ceremonies for this highest honour in Scottish Rite Masonry.

## THE MASTER OF THE 33 DEGREES

Albert Pike (1809–92) pursued a military career, and his service as a general in the Confederate States Army is commemorated by a statue in Judiciary Square, Washington DC. He is also remembered as an illustrious Freemason, whose book *Morals and Dogma* (1871) became the keystone of Scottish Rite Freemasonry in the USA. Pike is buried at a location that plays a key

*Albert Pike*

role in *The Lost Symbol*, the House of the Temple on Sixteenth Street NW, Washington DC, where Mal'akh is raised to the 33rd degree of Masonry in the book's opening chapter. Until 1974, a copy of *Morals and Dogma* was given to every Scottish Rite initiate, but the book was eventually deemed too advanced for the organisation's new members. The book was never meant to be available to the public, and older editions still bear the phrase: 'ESOTERIC BOOK, FOR SCOTTISH RITE USE ONLY; TO BE RETURNED UPON WITHDRAWAL OR DEATH OF RECIPIENT'. In *Morals and Dogma*, Pike explains the significance of each of the degrees of Scottish Rite Freemasonry up to the 32nd. He does not include details of the 33rd degree, and no reliable documentation of the ritual has ever been published, although many, including Dan Brown, suggest that the candidate must drink wine from a human skull, while swearing the following oath: 'May this wine I now drink become a deadly poison to me, as the Hemlock juice drunk by Socrates, should I ever knowingly or willfully violate the same.' After this chilling oath, a Mason dressed as a skeleton embraces the candidate, who says, 'And may these cold arms forever encircle me should I ever knowingly or wilfully violate the same.'

The following extracts are from two chapters of Pike's *Morals and Dogma*.

### Chapter IV: Secret Master

MASONRY is a succession of allegories, the mere vehicles of great lessons in morality and philosophy. You will more fully appreciate its spirit, its object, its purposes, as you advance in the different Degrees, which you will find to constitute a great, complete, and harmonious system.

If you have been disappointed in the first three Degrees, *as you have received them*, and if it has seemed to you that the performance has not come up to the promise, that the lessons of morality are not new, and the scientific instruction is but rudimentary, and the symbols are imperfectly explained, remember that the ceremonies and lessons of those Degrees have been for ages more and more accommodating themselves, by curtailment and sinking into commonplace, to the often limited memory and capacity of the Master and Instructor, and to the intellect and needs of the Pupil and Initiate; that they have come to us from an age when symbols were used, not to *reveal* but to *conceal*; when the commonest learning was confined to a select few, and the simplest principles of morality seemed newly discovered truths; and that these antique and simple Degrees now stand like the broken columns of a roofless Druidic temple, in their rude and mutilated greatness; in many parts, also, corrupted by time, and disfigured by modern additions and absurd interpretations. They are but the entrance to the great Masonic Temple, the triple columns of the portico.

You have taken the first step over its threshold, the first step toward the inner sanctuary and heart of the temple. You are in the path that leads up the slope of the mountain of Truth; and it depends upon your secrecy, obedience, and fidelity, whether you will advance or remain stationary.

Imagine not that you will become indeed a Mason by learning what is commonly called the "work," or even by becoming familiar with our traditions. Masonry has a history, a literature, a philosophy. Its allegories and traditions will teach you much; but much is to be sought elsewhere. The streams of learning that now flow full and broad must be followed to their heads in the springs that well up in the remote past, and you will there find the origin and meaning of Masonry.

A few rudimentary lessons in architecture, a few universally admitted maxims of morality, a few unimportant traditions, whose real meaning is unknown or misunderstood, will no longer satisfy the earnest inquirer after Masonic truth. Let whoso is content with these, seek to climb no higher. He who desires to understand the harmonious and beautiful proportions of Freemasonry must read, study, reflect, digest, and discriminate. The true Mason is an ardent seeker after knowledge; and he knows that both books and the antique symbols of Masonry are vessels which come down to us full-freighted with the intellectual riches of the Past; and that in the lading of these argosies is much that sheds light on the history of Masonry, and proves its claim to be acknowledged the benefactor of mankind, born in the very cradle of the race. [...]

To attain the truth, and to serve our fellows, our country, and mankind--this is the noblest destiny of man. Hereafter and all your life it is to be your object. If you desire to ascend to that destiny, advance! If you have other and less noble objects, and are contented with a lower flight, halt here! Let others scale the heights, and Masonry fulfill her mission.

If you will advance, gird up your loins for the struggle! For the way is long and toilsome. Pleasure, all smiles, will beckon you on the one hand, and Indolence will invite you to sleep among the flowers, upon the other. Prepare, by secrecy, obedience, and fidelity, to resist the allurements of both!

Secrecy is indispensable in a Mason of whatever Degree. It is the first and almost the only lesson taught to the Entered Apprentice. The obligations which we have each assumed toward every Mason that lives, requiring of us the performance of the most serious and onerous duties toward those personally unknown to us until they demand our aid,--duties that must be performed, even at the risk of life, or our solemn oaths be broken and violated, and we be branded as false Masons and faithless men, teach us how profound a folly it would be to betray our secrets to those who, bound to us by no tie of common obligation, might, by obtaining them, call on us in their extremity, when the urgency of the occasion should allow us no time for inquiry, and the peremptory mandate of our obligation compel us to do a brother's duty to a base impostor. [...]

In this Degree, my brother, you are especially to learn the duty of obedience to that law. There is one true and original law, conformable to reason and to nature, diffused over all, invariable, eternal, which calls to the fulfillment of duty, and to abstinence from injustice, and calls with that irresistible voice which is felt in all its authority wherever it is heard. [...]

Masonry is useful to all men: to the learned, because it affords them the opportunity of exercising their talents upon subjects eminently worthy of their attention; to the illiterate, because it offers them important instruction;

to the young, because it presents them with salutary precepts and good examples, and accustoms them to reflect on the proper mode of living; to the man of the world, whom it furnishes with noble and useful recreation; to the traveller, whom it enables to find friends and brothers in countries where else he would be isolated and solitary; to the worthy man in misfortune, to whom it gives assistance; to the afflicted, on whom it lavishes consolation; to the charitable man, whom it enables to do more good, by uniting with those who are charitable like himself; and to all who have souls capable of appreciating its importance, and of enjoying the charms of a friendship founded on the same principles of religion, morality, and philanthropy.

A Freemason, therefore, should be a man of honor and of conscience, preferring his duty to everything beside, even to his life; independent in his opinions, and of good morals; submissive to the laws, devoted to humanity, to his country, to his family; kind and indulgent to his brethren, friend of all virtuous men, and ready to assist his fellows by all means in his power.

Thus will you be faithful to yourself, to your fellows, and to God, and thus will you do honor to the name and rank of SECRET MASTER; which, like other Masonic honors, degrades if it is not deserved.

Pike's work continues in this vein, describing at length the significance of each of the degrees of the Scottish Rite until the work's final chapter:

## *Chapter XXXII: Sublime Prince of the Royal Secret*

THE Occult Science of the Ancient Magi was concealed under the shadows of the Ancient Mysteries: it was imperfectly revealed or rather disfigured by the Gnostics: it is guessed at under the obscurities that cover the pretended crimes of the Templars; and it is found enveloped in enigmas that seem impenetrable, in the Rites of the Highest Masonry.

Magism was the Science of Abraham and Orpheus, of Confucius and Zoroaster. It was the dogmas of this Science that were engraven on the tables of stone by Hanoch and Trismegistus. Moses purified and re-*veiled* them, for that is the meaning of the word *reveal*. He covered them with a new veil, when he made of the Holy Kabalah the exclusive heritage of the people of Israel, and the inviolable Secret of its priests. The Mysteries of Thebes and Eleusis preserved among the nations some symbols of it, already altered, and the mysterious key whereof was lost among the instruments of an ever-growing superstition.

Jerusalem, the murderess of her prophets, and so often prostituted to the false gods of the Syrians and Babylonians, had at length in its turn lost the Holy Word, when a Prophet announced to the Magi by the consecrated Star of Initiation, came to rend asunder the worn veil of the old Temple, in order to give the Church a new tissue of legends and symbols, that still and ever conceals from the Profane, and ever preserves to the Elect the same truths.

It was the remembrance of this scientific and religious Absolute, of this doctrine that is summed up in a word, of this Word, in fine, alternately lost and found again, that was transmitted to the Elect of all the Ancient Initiations: it was this same remembrance, preserved, or perhaps profaned in the celebrated Order of the Templars, that became for all the secret associations, of the Rose-Croix, of the Illuminati, and of the Hermetic Freemasons, the reason of their strange rites, of their signs more or less conventional, and, above all, of their mutual devotedness and of their power.

The Gnostics caused the Gnosis to be proscribed by the Christians, and the official Sanctuary was closed against the high initiation. Thus the Hierarchy of Knowledge was compromitted by the violences of usurping ignorance, and the disorders of the Sanctuary are reproduced in the State; for always, willingly or unwillingly, the King is sustained by the Priest, and it is from the eternal Sanctuary of the Divine instruction that the Powers of the Earth, to insure themselves durability, must receive their consecration and their force.

The Hermetic Science of the early Christian ages, cultivated also by Geber, Alfarabius, and others of the Arabs, studied by the Chiefs of the Templars, and embodied in certain symbols of the higher Degrees of Freemasonry, may be accurately defined as the Kabalah in active realization, or the Magic of Works. It has three analogous Degrees, religious, philosophical, and physical realization. [...]

Measure a corner of the Creation, and multiply that space in proportional progression, and the entire Infinite will multiply its circles filled with universes, which will pass in proportional segments between the ideal and elongating branches of your Compass. Now suppose that from any point whatever of the Infinite above you a hand holds another Compass or a Square, the lines of the Celestial triangle will necessarily meet those of the Compass of Science, to form the Mysterious Star of Solomon.

All hypotheses scientifically probable are the last gleams of the twilight of knowledge, or its last shadows. Faith begins where Reason sinks exhausted. Beyond the human Reason is the Divine Reason, to our feebleness the great Absurdity, the Infinite Absurd, which confounds us and which we believe. For the Master, the Compass of Faith is *above* the Square of Reason; but *both* rest upon the Holy Scriptures and combine to form the Blazing Star of Truth.

All eyes do not see alike. Even the visible creation is not, for all who look upon it, of one form and one color. Our brain is a book printed within and without, and the two writings are, with all men, more or less confused.

The primary tradition of the single revelation has been preserved under the name of the "Kabalah," by the Priesthood of Israel. The Kabalistic doctrine, which was also the dogma of the Magi and of Hermes, is contained in the Sepher Yetsairah, the Sohar, and the Talmud. According to that doctrine, the Absolute is the Being, in which The Word Is, the Word that is the utterance and expression of being and life.

Magic is that which it is; it is by itself, like the mathematics; for it is the exact and absolute science of Nature and its laws.

Magic is the science of the Ancient Magi: and the Christian religion, which has imposed silence on the lying oracles, and put an end to the prestiges of the false Gods, itself reveres those Magi who came from the East, guided by a Star, to adore the Saviour of the world in His cradle.

Tradition also gives these Magi the title of *"Kings;"* because initiation into Magism constitutes a genuine royalty; and because the grand art of the Magi is styled by all the Adepts, *"The Royal Art,"* or the *Holy Realm* or *Empire, Sanctum Regnum.*

The Star which guided them is that same Blazing Star, the image whereof we find in all initiations. To the Alchemists it is the sign of the Quintessence; to the Magists, the Grand Arcanum; to the Kabalists, the Sacred Pentagram. The study of this Pentagram could not but lead the Magi to the knowledge of the New Name which was about to raise itself above all names, and cause all creatures capable of adoration to bend the knee.

Magic unites in one and the same science, whatsoever Philosophy can possess that is most certain, and Religion of the Infallible and the Eternal. It perfectly and incontestably reconciles these two terms that at first blush seem so opposed to each other; faith and reason, science and creed, authority and liberty.

It supplies the human mind with an instrument of philosophical and religious certainty, exact as the mathematics, and accounting for the infallibility of the mathematics themselves.

Thus there is an Absolute, in the matters of the Intelligence and of Faith. The Supreme Reason has not left the gleams of the human understanding to vacillate at hazard. There is an incontestable verity, there is an infallible method of knowing this verity, and by the knowledge of it, those who accept it as a rule may give their will a sovereign power that will make them the masters of all inferior things and of all errant spirits; that is to say, will make them the Arbiters and Kings of the World.

Science has its nights and its dawns, because it gives the intellectual world a life which has its regulated movements and its progressive phases. It is with Truths, as with the luminous rays: nothing of what is concealed is lost; but also, nothing of what is discovered is absolutely new. God has been pleased to give to Science, which is the reflection of His Glory, the Seal of His Eternity.

It is not in the books of the Philosophers, but in the religious symbolism of the Ancients, that we must look for the footprints of Science, and re-discover the

Mysteries of Knowledge. The Priests of Egypt knew, better than we do, the laws of movement and of life. They knew how to temper or intensify action by re-action; and readily foresaw the realization of these effects, the causes of which they had determined. The Columns of Seth, Enoch, Solomon, and Hercules have symbolized in the Magian traditions this universal law of the Equilibrium; and the Science of the Equilibrium or balancing of Forces had led the Initiates to that of the universal gravitation around the centres of Life, Heat, and Light. [...]

Return now, with us, to the Degrees of the Blue Masonry, and for your last lesson, receive the explanation of one of their Symbols.

You see upon the altar of those Degrees the SQUARE and the COMPASS, and you remember how they lay upon the altar in each Degree.

The SQUARE is an instrument adapted for plane surfaces only, and therefore appropriate to Geometry, or measurement of the Earth, which appears to be, and was by the Ancients supposed to be, a plane. The COMPASS is an instrument that has relation to spheres and spherical surfaces, and is adapted to spherical trigonometry, or that branch of mathematics which deals with the Heavens and the orbits of the planetary bodies.

The SQUARE, therefore, is a natural and appropriate Symbol of this Earth and the things that belong to it, are of it, or concern it. The COMPASS is an equally natural and appropriate Symbol of the Heavens, and of all celestial things and celestial natures.

You see at the beginning of this reading [on page 212], an old Hermetic Symbol, copied from the "MATERIA PRIMA" of Valentinus, printed at Franckfurt, in 1613, with a treatise entitled "AZOTH." Upon it you see a Triangle upon a Square, both of these contained in a circle; and above this, standing upon a dragon, a human body, with two arms only, but two heads, one male and the other female. By the side of the male head is the Sun, and by that of the female head, the Moon, the crescent within the circle of the full moon. And the hand on the *male* side holds a *Compass*, and that on the *female* side, a *Square*.

[...]

The COMPASS, therefore, as the Symbol of the *Heavens*, represents the spiritual, intellectual, and moral portion of this double nature of Humanity; and the SQUARE, as the Symbol of the *Earth*, its material, sensual, and baser portion. [...]

It is enough for us to know, what Masonry teaches, that we are not all mortal; that the Soul or Spirit, the intellectual and reasoning portion of ourself, is our Very Self, is not subject to decay and dissolution, but is simple and immaterial, survives the death of the body, and is capable of immortality; that it is also *capable* of improvement and advancement, of increase of knowledge of the things that are divine, of becoming wiser and better, and more and more worthy of immortality; and that to become so, and to help to improve and benefit others and all our race, is the noblest ambition and highest glory that we can entertain and attain unto, in this momentary and imperfect life. [...]

The ROYAL SECRET, of which you are Prince, if you are a true Adept, if knowledge seems to you advisable, and Philosophy is, for you, radiant with a divine beauty, is that which the Sohar terms *The Mystery of the* BALANCE. It is the Secret of the UNIVERSAL EQUILIBRIUM:--

--Of that Equilibrium in the Deity, between the Infinite Divine WISDOM and the Infinite Divine POWER, from which result the Stability of the Universe, the unchangeableness of the Divine Law, and the Principles of Truth, Justice, and Right which are a part of it; and the Supreme Obligation of the Divine Law upon all men, as superior to all other law, and forming a part of all the laws of men and nations.

--Of that Equilibrium also, between the Infinite Divine JUSTICE and the Infinite Divine MERCY, the result of which is the Infinite Divine EQUITY, and the Moral Harmony or Beauty of the Universe. By it the endurance of created and imperfect natures in the presence of a Perfect Deity is made possible; and for Him, also, as for us, to love is better than to hate, and Forgiveness is wiser than Revenge or Punishment.

--Of that Equilibrium between NECESSITY and LIBERTY, between the action of the DIVINE Omnipotence and the Free-will of man, by which vices and base actions, and ungenerous thoughts and words are crimes and wrongs, justly punished by the law of cause and consequence, though nothing in the Universe can happen or be done contrary to the will of God; and without which co-existence of Liberty and Necessity, of Free-will in the creature and Omnipotence in the Creator, there could be no religion, nor any law of right and wrong, or merit and demerit, nor any justice in human punishments or penal laws.

--Of that Equilibrium between Good and Evil, and Light and Darkness in the world, which assures us that all is the work of the Infinite Wisdom and of an Infinite Love; and that there is no rebellious demon of Evil, or Principle of Darkness co-existent and in eternal controversy with God, or the Principle of Light and of Good: by attaining to the knowledge of which equilibrium we can, through Faith, see that the existence of Evil, Sin, Suffering, and Sorrow in the world is consistent with the Infinite Goodness as well as with the Infinite Wisdom of the Almighty. [...]

--Of that Equilibrium between Authority and Individual Action which constitutes Free Government, by settling on immutable foundations Liberty with Obedience to Law, Equality with Subjection to Authority, and Fraternity with Subordination to the Wisest and the Best: and of that Equilibrium between the Active Energy of the Will of the Present, expressed by the Vote of the People, and the Passive Stability and Permanence of the Will of the Past, expressed in constitutions of government, written or unwritten, and in the laws and customs, gray with age and sanctified by time, as precedents and authority; which is represented by the arch resting on the two columns, Jachin and Boaz, that stand at the portals of the Temple builded by Wisdom, on one of which Masonry sets the celestial Globe, symbol of the spiritual part of our composite nature, and on the other the terrestrial Globe, symbol of the material part.

--And, finally, of that Equilibrium, possible in ourselves, and which Masonry incessantly labors to accomplish in its Initiates, and demands of its Adepts and Princes (else unworthy of their titles), between the Spiritual and Divine and the Material and Human in man; between the Intellect, Reason, and Moral Sense on one side, and the Appetites and Passions on the other, from which result the Harmony and Beauty of a well-regulated life. [...]

And as in each Triangle of Perfection, one is three and three are one, so man is one, though of a double nature; and he attains the purposes of his being only when the two natures that are in him are in just equilibrium; and his life is a success only when it too is a harmony, and beautiful, like the great Harmonies of God and the Universe.

Such, my Brother, is the TRUE WORD of a Master Mason; such the true ROYAL SECRET, which makes possible, and shall at length make real, the HOLY EMPIRE of true Masonic Brotherhood.

GLORIA DEI EST CELARE VERBUM [It is the glory of god to conceal a thing.]

AMEN.

# THE YORK RITE

Another, completely separate, strand of Masonic tradition is that of the 'York Rite'. The York Rite consists of a modest 10 degrees grouped within three individual, separate rites, the final degree of which confirms the link between the Masons and the Knights Templar.

## Rite No. 1: The Capitular Degrees

The Capitular Degrees are four degrees controlled by the Royal Arch Chapter. 'Capitular' refers to the construction phases of Solomon's Temple.

### Mark Master

This degree relates to the story of the Fellowcraft of the quarry and their role in the building of the Temple.

### Past Master (Virtual)

This degree is conferred because ancient custom required that a Mason must be a Past Master in order to be exalted to the Royal Arch. In some Grand Jurisdictions this degree is conferred upon all sitting Masters of the Blue Lodge.

### Most Excellent Master

This degree is centred on the dedication of the Temple after its completion, particularly the consecration of the

Sanctum Sanctorum and the descent of the Host into the Temple. It is complementary to the Mark Master degree and completes the symbolic lessons introduced in that degree.

### The Royal Arch

The completion of the Master Mason degree and the summit of the original degrees of the Blue Lodge as practised in the Antients Lodges of England before 1820.

## Rite No. 2: The Cryptic Degrees

The Cryptic Degrees are three degrees controlled by the Select Masters Council. Only the first two degrees are regularly worked; the third is worked as an honorary degree, not being required as a requisite for membership in the Council.

### Royal Master

The degree centres on the Fellowcraft Masons who were artificers fabricating the fittings and furniture of the Temple. It is unusual in that the first part of the degree depicts events taking place before the death of the Grand Master Hiram Abiff, and the last part depicts events occurring after his death.

### Select Master

The degree centres on the construction and furnishing of a Secret Vault beneath the Sanctum Sanctorum of the

Temple, and the deposition of those secrets pertaining to the Craft by the three ancient Grand Masters of the Craft.

### Super Excellent Master

The degree centres on the events leading to the destruction of Jerusalem and the Temple at the hands of the Chaldeans. This degree is an honorary one.

## Rite No. 3: The Chivalric Orders

The Chivalric Orders are three orders culminating in the grade of Knight Templar, and controlled by that body. This body is markedly different from its foreign counterparts, in that it exhibits a paramilitary structure and outlook on Masonry, being the only branch of Masonry in the world that is uniformed. It requires its members to be professed Christians, and this has led to condemnation from other Masonic bodies and organisations, claiming that the body is Christian rather than Masonic.

### Illustrious Order of the Red Cross

Elements of this order were practised in Ancient Lodges before the final form of the Master Mason degree came into use. It is still practised in the full ceremonial form by the Knight Masons of Ireland and the Knight Masons of the United States, and as the Red Cross of Babylon in the English Order of the Allied Masonic Degrees.

### Order of Malta

This order requires the Mason to profess and practise the Christian faith. The order is centred on allegorical elements of the Knights of Malta, inheritors of the medieval Knights Hospitaller.

### Order of the Temple

This order is meant to rekindle the spirit of the medieval Knights Templar's devotion and self-sacrifice to Christianity.

*Dress of a Knight Templar*

## ◆ CHAPTER VI ◆

# The Illuminati:
# The Masonic Connection

The Illuminati have been the object of speculation by conspiracy theorists for hundreds of years. As the letters in Chapter III show, George Washington himself was more than merely aware of their existence, for he states 'It was not my intention to doubt that the Doctrines of the Illuminati, and principles of Jacobinism had not spread in the United States. On the contrary, *no one is more truly satisfied of this fact than I am.*' This last phrase has led some to believe that Washington, who we know was a Master Mason, was also a member of the Illuminati or of an affiliated movement in the USA at the time.

The Illuminati were a secret society founded by Adam Weishaupt in Bavaria on 1 May 1776. The movement was grounded in the Enlightenment thinking of Weishaupt's contemporary Germany, which showed a marked tendency away from religious and towards secular institutions. The Illuminati gathered 2,000 members, including the German literati Johann Wolfgang von Goethe and Johann Gottfried Herder, as well as the then dukes of Weimar and Gotha. The society, along with all other secret societies, was banned by the new ruler of Bavaria, Karl Theodor, in 1784 and was forced underground. Little is known about the society from this point onwards – many believe it was disbanded, but others take the view that the Illuminati persevered and simply became more clandestine in their workings.

Adam Weishaupt was a practising Freemason and he used elements of Masonic symbolism in the rituals of the Illuminati. Many have drawn the link between the Masons and the Illuminati, but a particularly revealing work is John Robison's *Proofs of a Conspiracy against all the Religions and Governments of Europe, carried on in the Secret Meetings of Free-Masons, Illuminati and Reading Societies, etc., collected from good authorities* (1797). This is the book that Washington was sent by John Snyder (see Washington's Masonic correspondence in Chapter III), to whom he wrote in reply: 'I have heard much of the nefarious and dangerous plan, and doctrines of the Illuminati,

but never saw the Book until you were pleased
to send it to me.' In this work, published just
thirteen years after the Illuminati were officially
disbanded, Robison claims that the society is still
working underground and draws specific links
between the Illuminati and the Freemasons:

### Introduction

BEING AT a friend's house in the country during some
part of the summer 1795, I there saw a volume of a
German periodical work called *Religions Begebenheiten, i.e.*
Religious Occurrences; in which there was an account
of the various schisms in the Fraternity of Free Masons,
with frequent allusions to the origin and history of that
celebrated association. This account interested me a good
deal, because, in my early life, I had taken some part in
the occupations (shall I call them) of Free Masonry; and
having chiefly frequented the Lodges on the Continent, I
had learned many doctrines, and seen many ceremonials,
which have no place in the simple system of Free Masonry
which obtains in this country. I had also remarked that
the whole was much more the object of reflection and
thought than I could remember it to have been among my
acquaintances at home. There, I had seen a Mason Lodge
considered merely as a pretext for passing an hour or two
in a fort of decent conviviality, not altogether void of some
rational occupation. I had sometimes heard of differences

of doctrines or of ceremonies, but in terms which marked them as mere frivolities. But, on the Continent, I found them matters of serious concern and debate. [...]

My masonic rank admitted me to a very elegant entertainment in the female *Loge de la Fidélité*, where every ceremonial was composed in the highest degree of elegance, and every thing conducted with the most delicate respect for our fair sisters, and the old song of brotherly love was chanted in the most refined strain of sentiment. I do not suppose that the Parisian Free Masonry of forty-five degrees could give me more entertainment. I had profited so much by it, that I had the honor of being appointed the Brother-orator. In this office I gave such satisfaction, that a worthy Brother sent me at midnight a box, which he committed to my care, as a person far advanced in masonic science, zealously attached to the order, and therefore a fit depositary of important writings. I learned next day that this gentleman had found it convenient to leave the empire in a hurry, but taking with him the funds of an establishment of which her Imperial Majesty had made him the manager. I was desired to keep these writings till he should see me again. I obeyed. About ten years afterward I saw the gentleman on the street in Edinburgh, conversing with a foreigner. As I passed by him, I saluted him softly in the Russian language, but without stopping, or even looking him in the face. He coloured, but made no return. I endeavoured in vain to meet with him, intending to make a proper return for much civility and kindness which I had received from him in his own country.

I now considered the box as accessible to myself, and opened it. I found it to contain all the degrees of the *Parfait Maçon Écossois*, with the Rituals, Catechisms, and Instructions, and also four other degrees of Free Masonry, as cultivated in the Parisian Lodges. I have kept them with all care, and mean to give them to some respectable Lodge. But as I am bound by no engagement of any kind, I hold myself as at liberty to make such use of them as may be serviceable to the public, without enabling any uninitiated person to enter the Lodges of these degrees. [...]

German Masonry appeared a very serious concern, and to be implicated with other subjects with which I had never suspected it to have any connection. I saw it much connected with many occurrences and schisms in the Christian church; I saw that the Jesuits had several times interfered in it; and that most of the exceptionable innovations and dissentions had arisen about the time that the order of *Loyola* was suppressed; so that it should seem that these intriguing brethren had attempted to maintain their influence by the help of Free Masonry. I saw it much disturbed by the mystical whims of J. Behmen and Swedenborg--by the fanatical and knavish doctrines of the modern Rosycrucians--by Magicians--Magnetisers--Exorcists, &c. And I observed that these different sects reprobated each other, as not only maintaining erroneous opinions, but even inculcating opinions which were contrary to the established religions of Germany, and contrary to the principles of the civil establishments. [...]

It has accordingly happened that the homely Free

Masonry imported from England has been totally changed in every country of Europe, either by the imposing ascendancy of French brethren, who are to be found every where, ready to instruct the world; or by the importation of the doctrines, and ceremonies, and ornaments of the Parisian Lodges. Even England, the birth-place of Masonry, has experienced the French innovations; and all the repeated injunctions, admonitions, and reproofs of the old Lodges cannot prevent those in different parts of the kingdom from admitting the French novelties, full of tinsel and glitter, and high-sounding titles.

Were this all, the harm would not be great. But long before good opportunities had occurred for spreading the refinements on the simple Free Masonry of England, the Lodges in France had become places of very serious discussion, where opinions in morals, in religion, and in politics, had been promulgated and maintained with a freedom and a keenness, of which we in this favored land have no adequate notion, because we are unacquainted with the restraints, which, in other countries, are laid on ordinary conversation. In consequence of this, the French innovations in Free Masonry were quickly followed in all parts of Europe by the admission of similar discussions, although in direct opposition to a standing rule, and a declaration made to every newly received Brother, "that nothing touching the religion or government shall ever be spoken of in the Lodge." But the Lodges in other countries followed the example of France, and have frequently become the rendezvous of innovators in religion and politics, and other disturbers of the public peace. In short, I have found that the covert of a Mason Lodge had been employed in every country for venting and propagating sentiments in religion and politics, that could not have circulated in public without exposing the author to great danger. I found, that this impunity had gradually encouraged men of licentious principles to become more bold, and to teach doctrines subversive of all our notions of morality--of all our confidence in the moral government of the universe--of all our hopes of improvement in a future state of existence--and of all satisfaction and contentment with our present life, so long as we live in a state of civil subordination. I have been able to trace these attempts, made through a course of fifty years, under the specious pretext of enlightening the world by the torch of philosophy, and of dispelling the clouds of civil and religious superstition which keep the nations of Europe in darkness and slavery. I have observed these doctrines gradually diffusing and mixing with all the different systems of Free Masonry; till, at last, AN ASSOCIATION HAS BEEN FORMED for the express purpose of ROOTING OUT ALL THE RELIGIOUS ESTABLISHMENTS, AND OVERTURNING ALL THE EXISTING GOVERNMENTS OF EUROPE. I have seen this Association exerting itself zealously and systematically, till it has become almost irresistible: And I have seen that the most active leaders in the French Revolution were members of this Association, and conducted their first movements according to its principles, and by means of its instructions and assistance, *formerly requested and obtained:* And, lastly, I have seen that this Association still exists, still works in secret, and that not only several appearances among ourselves show that its emissaries are endeavoring to propagate their detestable doctrines among us, but that the Association has Lodges in Britain corresponding with the mother Lodge at Munich ever since 1784. [...]

## Chapter I: Schisms in Free Masonry

[...] In 1743, a Baron Hunde, a gentleman of honorable character and independent fortune, was in Paris, and got acquainted with the Earl of Kilmarnock and some other gentlemen who were about the Pretender, and learned from them that they had some wonderful secrets in their Lodges. He was admitted, through the medium of that nobleman, and of a Lord Clifford, and his Masonic patent was signed *George* (said to be the signature of Kilmarnock). Hunde had attached himself to the fortunes of the Pretender, in hopes (as he says himself) of rising in the world under his protection. The mighty secret was this. "When the Order of Knights Templars was abolished by Philip the Fair, and cruelly persecuted, some worthy persons escaped, and took refuge in the Highlands of Scotland, where they concealed themselves in caves. These persons possessed the true secrets of Masonry, which had always been in that Order, having been acquired by the Knights, during their services in the east, from the pilgrims whom they occasionally protected or delivered. The *Chevaliers de la Rose-Croix* continued to have the same duties as formerly, though robbed of their emoluments. In fine, every true Mason is a Knight Templar." [...]

## Chapter II: The Illuminati

[...] Of the zealous members of the Lodge Theodore the most conspicuous was Dr. Adam Weishaupt, Professor of Canon Law in the University of Ingolstadt. This person had been educated among the Jesuits; but the abolition of their order made him change his views, and from being their pupil, he became their most bitter enemy. He had acquired a high reputation in his profession, and was attended not only by those intended for the practice in the law-courts, but also by the young gentlemen at large, in their course of general education; and he brought numbers from the neighbouring states to this university, and gave a *ton* to the studies of the place. [...]

Weishaupt had long been scheming the establishment of an Association or Order, which, in time, should govern the world. In his first fervour and high expectations, he hinted to several Ex-Jesuits the probability of their recovering, under a new name, the influence which they formerly possessed, and of being again of great service to society, by directing the education of youth of distinction, now emancipated from all civil and religious prejudices. He prevailed on some to join him, but they all retracted but two. After this disappointment Weishaupt became the implacable enemy of the Jesuits; and his sanguine temper made him frequently lay himself open to their piercing eye, and drew on him their keenest resentment, and at last made him the victim of their enmity.

The Lodge Theodore was the place where the above-mentioned doctrines were most zealously propagated. But Weishaupt's emissaries had already procured the adherence of many other Lodges; and the Eclectic Masonry had been brought into vogue chiefly by their exertions at the Willemsbad convention. The Lodge Theodore was perhaps less guarded in its proceedings, for it became remarkable for the very bold sentiments in politics and religion which were frequently uttered in their harangues; and its members were noted for their zeal in making proselytes. Many bitter pasquinades, satires, and other offensive pamphlets were in secret circulation, and even larger works of very dangerous tendency, and several of them were traced to that Lodge. The Elector often expressed his disapprobation of such proceedings, and sent them kind messages, desiring them to be careful not to disturb the peace of the country, and particularly to recollect the solemn declaration made to every entrant into the Fraternity of Free Masons, "That no subject of religion or politics shall ever be touched on in the Lodge;" a declaration which alone could have procured his permission of any secret assembly whatever, and on the sincerity and honor of which he had reckoned when he gave his sanction to their establishment. But repeated accounts of the same kind increased the alarm, and the Elector ordered a judicial enquiry into the proceedings of the Lodge Theodore.

It was then discovered that this and several associated Lodges were the nursery or preparation-school for another Order of Masons, who called themselves the ILLUMINATED, and that the express aim of this Order was to abolish Christianity, and overturn all civil government. [...]

The Order of ILLUMINATI appears as an accessory to Free Masonry. It is in the Lodges of Free Masons that the Minervals are found, and there they are prepared for Illumination. They must have previously obtained the three English degrees. The founder says more. He says that his doctrines are the only true Free Masonry. He was the chief promoter of the *Eclectic System*. This he urged as the best method for getting information of all the explanations which have been given of the Masonic Mysteries. [...]

And have not their missionaries been among us, prying into our mysteries, and eager to learn from us what is true Free Masonry? It is in vain, therefore, to appeal to judges; they are no where to be found; all claim for themselves the sceptre of the Order; all indeed are on an equal footing. They obtained followers, not from their authenticity, but from their conduciveness to the end which they proposed, and from the importance of that end. It is by this scale that we must measure the mad and wicked explanations of the Rosycrucians, the Exorcists, and Cabalists. These are rejected by all good Masons, because incompatible with social happiness. Only such systems as promote this are retained. But alas, they are all sadly deficient, because they leave us under the dominion of political and religious prejudice; and they are as inefficient as the sleepy dose of an ordinary sermon.

But I have contrived an explanation which has every advantage; is inviting to Christians of every communion; gradually frees them from all religious prejudices; cultivates the social virtues; and animates them by a great, a feasible, and *speedy* prospect of universal happiness, in a state of liberty and moral equality, freed from the obstacles which subordination, rank, and riches, continually throw in our way. My explanation is accurate, and complete, my means are effectual, and irresistible. Our secret Association works in a way that nothing can withstand, *and man shall soon be free and happy.*

*The manner of Receiving the word from the* MASTER

## • CHAPTER VII •

# Masonic Songs and a Poem

he masons may seem a serious lot, but it's not all blood-curdling oaths and allegorical lessons, and at the closing of a Lodge meeting, it's traditional to sing one or more Masonic songs. Songs are also sometimes sung at the dinner, termed 'Festive Board', that traditionally follows each Masonic meeting. Once a year, the wives of Freemasons are invited to enter the Masonic lodge to dine with their partners, and there is a special, rather un-PC song that is sung to commemorate the occasion.

## THE Enter'd 'PRENTICES SONG

By our late BROTHER
Mr. MATTHEW BIRKHEAD, deceas'd.
To be sung when all grave Business is over, and with the MASTER's Leave.

COME let us prepare,
We Brothers that are
Assembled on merry Occasion:
Let's drink, laugh, and sing;
Our Wine has a Spring:
Here's a Health to an Accepted Mason.

The World is in pain
Our Secrets to gain,
And still let them wonder and gaze on;
They ne'er can divine
The Word or the Sign
Of a Free and an Accepted Mason.

'Tis This, and 'tis That,
They cannot tell What,
Why so many Great Men of the Nation
Should Aprons put on,
To make themselves one
With a Free and an Accepted Mason.

Great Kings, Dukes, and Lords,
Have laid by their Swords,
Our Myst'ry to put a good Grace on,
And ne'er been asham'd
To hear themselves nam'd
With a Free and an Accepted Mason.

Antiquity's Pride
We have on our side,
And it maketh Men just in their Station:
There's nought but what's good
To be understood
By a Free and an Accepted Mason.

Then join Hand in Hand,
T'each other firm stand,
Let's be merry, and put a bright Face on:
What Mortal can boast
So NOBLE A TOAST,
As a Free and an Accepted Mason?

## A New SONG, by Benjamin Franklin

WHAT though they call us Masons Fools,
We prove by Geometry and Rules,
We've Arts are taught in all our Schools;
They charge us falsely then.
We make it plainly to appear,
By our Behaviour every where
That where you meet a Mason, there
You meet a Gentleman.

'Tis true we once have charged been
With Disobedience to our Queen;
But after Monarchs plain have seen,
The Secrets they have sought.

We hatch no Plots against the State,
Nor 'gainst great Men in Power prate
But all that's generous, good and great
Is daily by us taught.

What noble Structures do we see
By ancient Brethren raised be!
The World's surpriz'd, and shall not we
Then honour Masonry?
Let those that do despise the Art
Live in a Cave in some Desart,
And herd with beasts from Men apart,
For their Stupidity.

View but those Savage Nations, where
No Masonry did e'er appear,
What strange unpolish'd Brutes they are!
Then honour Masonry.
It makes us courteous, easy, free,
Generous, honourable, and gay;
What other Art the like can say?
Here's a Health to Masonry.

## Installation Ode

MUSIC – 'Rule Britannia.'

WHEN earth's foundation first was laid,
By the Almighty Artist's hand;

'Twas then our perfect, our perfect laws were made,
Established by his strict command.

Hail! mysterious, Hail, glorious Masonry!
That makes us ever great and free.
In vain mankind for shelter sought,
In vain from place to place did roam,
Until from heaven, from heaven he was taught
To plan, to build, to fix his home.

Hail! Mysterious, Hail, glorious Masonry!
That makes us ever great and free.

Illustrious hence we date our Art,
And now in beauteous piles appear,
We shall to endless, to endless time impart,
How worthy and how great we are.

Hail! mysterious [...]

Nor we less fam'd for every tie,
By which the human thought is bound;
*Love, truth* and *friendship*, and friendship socially,
Join all our hearts and hands around.

Hail! mysterious [...]

Our actions still by Virtue blest,
And to our precepts ever true,

The world admiring, admiring shall request
To learn, and our bright paths pursue.

Hail! mysterious, Hail, glorious Masonry!
That makes us ever great and free.

## On Consecration of a Lodge

MUSIC – 'God save the King.'

HAIL, Masonry divine!
Glory of ages, shine!
Long may'st thou reign:
Where'er thy Lodges stand,
May they have great conmmand
And always grace the land.
Thou art divine!

Great fabrics still arise,
And grace the azure skies;
Great are thy schemes;
Thy noble orders are
Matchless, beyond compare;
No art with thee can share.
Thou art divine!

Hiram, the architect,
Did all the Craft direct
How they should build.

Sol'mon, great Israel's king,
Did mighty blessings bring,
And left us room to sing,
Hail, royal art!

## A song sung at Ladies' nights

THE Ladies claim right
To come to our Light,
Since the apron they say is their bearing;
Can they subject their will,
Can they keep their tongues still,
And let talking be changed into hearing?

This difficult task
Is the *least* we can ask,
To secure us on sundry occasions;
When with this they comply,
Our utmost we'll try
To raise Lodges for Lady Freemasons!

Till this can be done,
Must each Brother be mum,
Though the fair one should wheedle and teaze on;
Be just, true and kind;
But still bear in mind
At all times, that you are a Freemason.

## The Mason's Adieu

Words by ROBBIE BURNS.
AIR — Bonny Doon.

ADIEU, a heart warm, fond adieu,
Ye brothers of our mystic tie;
Ye favored and enlighten'd few,
Companions of my social joy;
Though I to foreign lands must hie,
Pursuing fortune's slipp'ry ba';
With melting heart and brimful eye,
I'll mind you still when far awa'.

Oft have I met your social band,
To spend a cheerful festive night,
Oft honor'd with supreme command,
Presiding o'er the sons of light:

And by that hieroglyphic bright,
Which none but craftsmen ever saw,
Strong mem'ry on my heart shall write,
Those happy scenes when far awa'.

May freedom, harmony and love,
Cement you in the grand design,
Beneath th' Omniscient Eye above,
The glorious Architect divine:

That you may keep th' unerring line,
Still guided by the plummet's law,
'Till order bright completely shine,
Shall be my prayer when far awa'.

And you, farewell, whose merits claim
Justly that highest badge to wear,
May heaven bless your noble name,
To Masonry and friendship dear:
My last request permit me then,
When yearly you're assembled a,
One round, I ask it with a tear,
To him, your friend that's far awa'.

And you, kind-hearted sisters, fair,
I sing farewell to all your charms –
Th' impression of your pleasing air
With rapture oft my bosom warms,
Alas! the social winter's night
No more returns while breath I draw
'Till sisters, brothers, all unite,
In that Grand Lodge that's far awa'.

*The Ceremony of Introducing a Intended Brother into the Lodge*

## ◆ APPENDIX I ◆

# Women and Freemasonry

The United Grand Lodge of England made its position on women Freemasons clear in a document it published in 1999, which stated that it did not admit women and that it did not recognise lodges that were 'irregular' in this way. Nevertheless there do exist a number of lodges that affiliate themselves with Freemasonry but accept women either exclusively or as well as men and, most interestingly, the earliest documents of Masonry suggest that women Freemasons are as old as the movement itself.

The text of one of the earliest documents of speculative Freemasonry, known as the York Manuscript No. 4, explains how the charge should be given to an Entered Apprentice: 'The elders taking the Booke, he or shee [sic] that is to be made Mason shall lay their hands thereon, and the charge shall be given.' Some Masonic authorities have suggested that 'shee' is a misprint for 'they', but the idea that women were initially not excluded from Freemasonry is backed up by another, even earlier manuscript, the *Regius*, which dates back to around 1390. The text encourages Masons to 'love togeder as syster and brothur'.

Secondly, there is a famous story that has passed into Masonic legend of how a woman, the Hon. Elizabeth St Leger (or, after her marriage, the Hon. Mrs Aldworth), was initiated as a Freemason. Brother Dudley Wright, in the Masonic magazine *The Builder*, explains:

'The Hon. Elizabeth St Leger was a daughter of the first Viscount Doneraile, a resident of Cork. Her father was a very zealous Freemason and, as was the custom in his time – the early part of the eighteenth century – held an occasional lodge in his own house, when he was assisted by members of his own family and any brethren in the immediate neighbourhood and visitors to Doneraile House. This lodge was duly warranted and held the number 150 on the Register of the Grand Lodge of Ireland.

'The story runs that one evening previous to the initiation of a gentleman named Coppinger, Miss St Leger hid herself in the room adjoining the one used as a lodgeroom. This room was at that time undergoing some alterations and Miss St Leger is said to have removed a brick from the partition with her scissors and through the aperture thus created witnessed the ceremony of initiation. What she saw appears to have disturbed her so thoroughly that she at once determined upon making her escape, but failed to elude the vigilance of the tyler, who, armed with a sword stood barring her exit. Her shrieks alarmed the members of the lodge, who came rushing to

*Order of the Eastern Star*

the spot, when they learned that she had witnessed the whole of the ceremony which had just been enacted. After a considerable discussion and yielding to the entreaties of her brother it was decided to admit her into the Order and she was duly initiated, and, in course of time, became the Master of the lodge.'

Today, there exist two groups of self-styled Women Freemasons in the UK: 'The Order of Women Freemasons', and 'The Honourable Fraternity of Ancient Freemasons'. Interestingly, the members of these orders still refer to each other as 'Brethren', leading to the rather incongruous title of the current head of the Order of Women Freemasons: The Most Worshipful Brother Brenda I. Fleming-Taylor.

Women Freemason groups also exist outside the UK; in the United States in the 1800s a Comasonic group (in other words, one including male and female members) was formed, called 'The Order of the Eastern Star'. Almost contemporaneously, another Comasonic organisation was formed, 'The Order of Amaranth'. Both organisations still exist and continue to initiate both men and women into Freemasonry to this day.

# Famous Freemasons

There are Freemasons famous enough to be household names in a huge variety of areas, from historical figures to popular entertainers. Their level of devotion to the Craft may vary, but every one of the following names has been initiated into the Masonic tradition and pledged an oath to Freemasonry that they can never revoke – although the membership of those marked by an asterisk (*) is disputed by some.

## English royalty

King George IV (1762–1830)
King William IV (1765–1837)
King Edward VII (1841–1910)
King Edward VIII (1894–1972)
King George VI (1895–1952)
Prince Philip, Duke of Edinburgh, husband and consort
of Queen Elizabeth II (1921–)
His Royal Highness Prince Edward the Duke of Kent,
Present Grand Master of the United Grand Lodge of
England (1935–)

## Other monarchs

Frederick the Great of Prussia (1712–86)
King Pedro I of Brazil and Pedro IV of Portugal
(1798–1834)
King Kalakaua of Hawaii (1836–91)
Habibullah Khan, Emir of Afghanistan (1872–1919)
King Hussein of Jordan (1935–99)

## Presidents of the USA

George Washington (1732–99), 1st President of the USA
James Monroe (1758–1831) 5th
Andrew Jackson (1767–1845) 7th
James Knox Polk (1795–1849) 11th
James Buchanan (1791–1868) 15th
Andrew Johnson (1808–75) 17th
James Abram Garfield (1831–81) 20th
William McKinley (1843–1901) 25th
Theodore Roosevelt (1858–1919) 26th
William Howard Taft (1857–1930) 27th
Warren Gamaliel Harding (1865–1923) 29th
Franklin Delano Roosevelt (1882–1945) 32nd
Harry S. Truman (1884–1972) 33rd
Lyndon Baines Johnson (EA) (1908–73) 36th
Gerald Ford (1913–2006) 38th

## Other presidents and prime ministers

Sir John Alexander Macdonald, 1st Canadian Prime
Minister (1815–91)
Viscount R. B. Bennett, former Canadian Prime Minister
(1870–1947)
Mustapha Kemal Ataturk, 1st President of Turkey
(1881–1938)
Sveinn Björnsson, 1st President of Iceland (1881–1952)

Eduard Beneš, former President of Czechoslovakia
(1884–1948)

Sir Winston Churchill, former Prime Minister of the UK
(1874–1965)

Salvador Allende, former President of Chile and head of
the *Unidad Popular* Marxist Party (1908–73)

## Politicians and statesmen

Benjamin Franklin, American statesman and inventor
(1706–90)

John Hancock, American merchant and signer of the
Declaration of Independence (1737–93)

DeWitt Clinton, former Mayor of New York
(1769–1828)

John Brown, American abolitionist (1800–59)

Fiorello H. Laguardia, three-time Mayor of New York and
namesake of the International Airport (1882–1947)

J. Edgar Hoover, American lawman and head of the FBI
(1895–1972)

Robert 'Bob' Dole (1923–)

Rev. Jesse Jackson, civil rights activist and Baptist
minister (1941–)

# Historical figures

Paul Revere, American Revolutionary war hero (1735–1818) – in fact, many believe that the Boston Tea Party was organised by the nearby Green Dragon Masonic lodge, of which Revere was a member.

John Paul Jones, Father of the American Navy (1747–92)

Admiral Lord Horatio Nelson (1758–1805), victor of Battle of Trafalgar*

Arthur, Duke of Wellington (1769–1852), British general who defeated Napoleon at Battle of Waterloo

Jerome, Joseph, Louis and Lucien Bonaparte, brothers of Napoleon (1769–1821), who was not a Mason

Simón Bolívar, liberator of South America (1783–1830)

Giuseppe Garibaldi, Italian revolutionary and liberator (1807–82)

Cecil Rhodes, colonial businessman and founder of the Rhodes Scholarship (1853–1902)

Field Marshal Sir Douglas Haig, First World War general (1861–1928)

# Businessmen and inventors

James Watt, inventor of the steam engine (1736–1819)

Joseph Michel and Jacques Étienne Montgolfier, inventors of the hot air balloon (1740–1810 and 1745–99)

John Loudon McAdam, Scottish engineer who developed
    tarmac (1756–1836)
Nathan Meyer Rothschild, founder of the family banking
    dynasty (1777–1836)*
Samuel Colt, American handgun manufacturer (1814–62)
Richard J. Gatling, inventor of the Gatling gun
    (1818–1903)
Sir Thomas Johnstone Lipton, Scottish tea merchant
    (1848–1931)
King Camp Gillette, inventor of the safety razor
    (1855–1932)
Henry Ford, American automobile manufacturer
    (1863–1947)
Walter P. Chrysler, American automobile manufacturer
    (1875–1940)
André Citroën, French-Jewish automobile manufacturer
    (1878–1935)
Colonel Harland Sanders, inventor of Kentucky Fried
    Chicken (1890–1980)
Steve Wozniak, co-founder of Apple Computers (1950–)

## Religious leaders

Geoffrey Fisher, Archbishop of Canterbury (1887–1972)
Sir Israel Brodie, Chief Rabbi of Great Britain and the
    Commonwealth (1895–1979)

## Philanthropists

Sir Joseph Banks, founder of Kew Gardens (1743–1820)
Jean-Henri Dunant, founder of the Red Cross
(1828–1910)
Dr T. J. Barnardo, founder of the London home for
orphaned boys (1845–1905)
Daniel Carter Beard, founder of the US Boy Scouts
movement (1850–1941)
Sir William Butlin, founder of Butlins holiday camps
and well-known philanthropist (1899–1980)

## Scientists

Erasmus Darwin, physician, botanist and grandfather of
Charles Darwin (1731–1802)
Edward Jenner, English doctor and inventor of
vaccination (1749–1823)
Sir Alexander Fleming, Scottish discoverer of penicillin
(1881–1955)

## Explorers

Captain Robert Falcon Scott, first Englishman to reach
the South Pole (1868–1912)
Sir Ernest Shackleton, Antarctic explorer (1874–1922)
Buzz Aldrin, second man on the moon (1930–)

## Actors and entertainers

Harry Houdini, American magician and escapologist
(1874–1926)
W. C. Fields, American comedian and entertainer
(1880–1946)
Al Jolson, American singer and actor who portrayed
black minstrels (1886–1950)
Oliver Hardy, American comedian, partner of Stan
Laurel (1892–1957)
Clark Gable, screen actor who starred in *Gone with the
Wind* (1901–60)
John Wayne, American film star (1907–79)
Mel Blanc, the voice behind Bugs Bunny, Daffy Duck
and others (1908–89)
Harry Corbett, English puppeteer of 'Sooty' shows
(1918–89)
Peter Sellers, English comic actor (1925–80)
Bob Monkhouse, English actor, TV presenter and
comedian (1928–2003)

Jim Davidson, English comedian (1953–)
Bradley Walsh, English comedian and TV actor (1960–)

## Composers and musicians

Thomas Augustine Arne, composer of 'Rule Britannia'
(1710–78)
Franz Josef Haydn, Austrian composer (1732–1809)
Wolfgang Amadeus Mozart, Austrian composer (1756–91)
Franz Liszt, Hungarian composer (1811–86)
Sir Arthur Seymore Sullivan, English composer of
operettas with fellow Mason Sir William S. Gilbert
(1842–1900)
Jean Sibelius, Finnish composer (1865–1957)
Irving Berlin, American songwriter and composer
(1888–1989)
William 'Count' Basie, American jazz pianist
(1904–84)
Nat King Cole, American singer and pianist (1917–65)

## Literary figures

Jonathan Swift, Irish poet and author of *Gulliver's Travels*
(1667–1745)

Alexander Pope, English satirical verse writer and translator of Homer (1688–1744)

Gotthold Ephraim Lessing, German Enlightenment playwright (1729–70)

Edward Gibbon, author of *The Decline and Fall of the Roman Empire* (1737–94)

Johann Wolfgang von Goethe, German writer and thinker (1749–1832)

Richard Brinsley Sheridan, playwright of Restoration comedy (1751–1816)

Robert Burns, Scottish poet (1759–96)

Sir Walter Scott, Scottish poet and writer of *Ivanhoe* (1771–1832)

Aleksandr Pushkin, Russian poet (1799–1837)

Anthony Trollope, English novelist (1815–82)

Mark Twain, American writer whose works include the Huckleberry Finn series (1835–1910)

Sir William S. Gilbert, English poet and playwright, collaborator with fellow Mason Arthur Sullivan (1836–1911)

Oscar Wilde, Anglo-Irish dramatist, poet and novelist (1854–1900)

Sir Arthur Conan Doyle, writer of the Sherlock Holmes stories (1859–1930)

Rudyard Kipling, English writer most famous for *The Jungle Book* (1865–1936)

P. G. Wodehouse, comic writer and creator of Jeeves and Wooster series (1881–1975)

## Artists and architects

Sir Christopher Wren, architect of many London
buildings including St Paul's Cathedral (1632–1723)

William Hogarth, English painter and social satirist
(1697–1764)

Sir John Soane, architect of the Bank of England
(1753–1837)

James Hoban, architect of the White House
(1758–1831)

Gutzon Borglum, sculptor of Mount Rushmore
(1867–1941)

Marc Chagall, Belorussian-born surrealist and
expressionist (1887–1985)

# Acknowledgements

Firstly, I am indebted to the amazing team at my publisher Profile Books, all of whom have been a tremendous help in preparing the book for publication. I would particularly like to thank Andrew Franklin and Paul Forty for dedicating their time to the project.

Secondly, I would like to thank the following people and organisations:

Paul Royster from the DigitalCommons team at the University of Nebraska, for *The Constitutions of the Freemason*.
Gary McElfresh and the Board of Trustees of Ancient Accepted Scottish Rite, Valley of Toledo.
The Grand Lodge of British Columbia and Yukon, for various Masonic images and information on famous Freemasons.